The Young Professional:

A Real World Survival Guide for the New College Graduate

ANDY J. SEMOTIUK

Cengage Learning PTR

☀️ CENGAGE
Learning·

Professional • Technical • Reference

Australia, Brazil, Japan, Korea, Mexico, Singapore, Spain, United Kingdom, United States

CENGAGE
Learning·

Professional • Technical • Reference

The Young Professional:
A Real World Survival
Guide for the New
College Graduate
Andy J. Semotiuk

Publisher and
General Manager,
Cengage Learning PTR:
Stacy L. Hiquet

Associate Director
of Marketing:
Sarah Panella

Manager of
Editorial Services:
Heather Talbot

Senior Marketing
Manager:
Mark Hughes

Senior Acquisitions
Editor:
Mitzi Koontz

Project and Copy
Editor:
Kate Shoup

Interior Layout:
Shawn Morningstar

Cover Designer:
Luke Fletcher

Indexer:
Larry Sweazy

Proofreader:
Megan Belanger

Printed in the United
States of America
1 2 3 4 5 6 7 15 14 13

For product information and technology assistance, contact us at **Cengage Learning Customer and Sales Support, 1-800-354-9706.**

For permission to use material from this text or product, submit all requests online at **cengage.com/permissions.**

Further permissions questions can be e-mailed to **permissionrequest@cengage.com.**

All trademarks are the property of their respective owners.

Library of Congress Control Number: 2013948720
ISBN-13: 978-1-285-86892-9
ISBN-10: 1-285-86892-7

Cengage Learning PTR
20 Channel Center Street
Boston, MA 02210
USA

Cengage Learning is a leading provider of customized learning solutions with office locations around the globe, including Singapore, the United Kingdom, Australia, Mexico, Brazil, and Japan. Locate your local office at: **international.cengage.com/region.**

Cengage Learning products are represented in Canada by Nelson Education, Ltd.

For your lifelong learning solutions, visit **cengageptr.com.**
Visit our corporate Web site at **cengage.com.**

Acknowledgments

In the 15th century, in a village near Nuremberg, Germany, there was a family named Dürer, with 18 children. The father was a shopkeeper and worked long hours to keep the family clothed and fed. Two of the sons, Albrecht and Albert, knew full well that their father could never afford to send either of them to the Nuremberg Art Academy, but nevertheless dreamed of studying there. So, the boys came up with a plan. They would toss a coin. The winner would study art at the academy, and the loser would work in the coal mines to support his brother. Then, in four years, the winner would support the other brother at the academy, either through the sale of his artwork or, if necessary, by laboring in the mines himself.

They tossed the coin, and Albrecht Dürer won. He went off to the Nuremberg Art Academy while Albert went down into the mines. Almost immediately, Albrecht became a sensation. By the end of his second year, Albrecht's etchings, woodcuts, and oils had surpassed those of all of his fellow students. By the time he graduated, his work had surpassed most of his professors and was becoming well-known throughout Europe.

After his graduation, the young artist returned to his village, and the Dürer family held a festive dinner to celebrate his triumphant homecoming. At the end of a long and memorable meal accompanied by music and laughter, Albrecht rose from his honored position at the head of the table to drink a toast to his beloved brother sitting at the other end. "Albert, my dear brother," Albrecht began. "Now it is your turn. Now you can go to Nuremberg, and I will take care of you." As Albrecht spoke, Albert lowered his head, shaking it from side to side as he muttered, "No, no, no." Then, interrupting his brother's toast, Albert stood and held up his twisted, deformed hands, mangled by years of work in the coal mines saying. "Look at these hands," Albert said. "I can't even hold up a glass to return your toast, much less go to Nuremberg to paint. For me it is too late."

It's been more than 450 years since then. Albrecht Dürer's art hangs in all the great museums of Europe. However, there is one painting particularly known the world over. Albrecht was so moved by his brother's sacrifice that he created a masterpiece in tribute to his brother and the hands that helped him. Today, that masterpiece, a pen-and-ink drawing, is known as *The Praying Hands*.

This story is as moving for me today as it was when I first heard Og Mandino relate it to a National Speakers Association convention on July 11, 1992, in Orlando, Florida. Though not completely accurate, I believe Mandino related the story in this way to remind us that nothing great is ever achieved without the help of others. The story reminds us that the success of any individual always involves the contributions of many. This was certainly the case for me when it came to writing this book.

I am indebted to all those who contributed to the success of this book. First among these was my dear wife Ann, who faithfully worked alongside me, supporting me in my efforts, and enabling me to find the time to do my writing. Without her help, this book would have gone nowhere. She is the "Albert" in my life.

My two children, Mark, my pride, and Natalie, my joy, gave me the motivation to complete this work. They were the "why" of this undertaking. Both offered me many valuable comments.

The individuals whose lives were included in the book deserve special gratitude. Since their names are already mentioned elsewhere I do not list them here.

Many people contributed their time and work to complete this project. Ilona Specht was a tireless and watchful assistant who edited, re-edited, and helped me when I ran out of energy to complete the task. Monica Stadnick and Nikki Riedmueller also helped with this editing work. Pat Nelson, Laurie Peck, and especially Steve Andrusiak were of enormous help. They made suggestions that improved the text. J.S. Mangat, Chrystyna Hnatiw, Wendy Duke, Monica Shymko, Monica Coplenas, Jodi Lea Rothwell, Stephanie Lee, Atisa Shirvani, Henry Wilman, Phyllis Arnold, and Steven Riznyk made useful recommendations. My two mastermind partners, John Evans and Ted Greer, also gave me ideas that found their way into this book as well.

Alex Brodsky Jr., Nand Shankar, and Dean Duke helped make the book a reality. The people at Hi-Tech Export in India, including Shreeja Dayanand and Naresh Dhingra, merit mention as well. Chinye Uwechue-Akpati, Greg Korneluk, Jerry Grod, Anne Prokopchuk, and Susan Dunn made welcome contributions. Ron Hansma helped me with the design of the book cover. Tami Anderson, Mary Denardo, and Karen from Girl Friday, as well as Ross Henderson, helped with editing.

I should also mention my colleagues at the law firms of Manning & Marder in Los Angeles and Hansma & Bristow in Edmonton, who supported me in my legal work over many years while I devoted some of my time to writing this book. I am also grateful to those individuals who lent me their support in my earlier efforts to publish these materials. Among them were Joe Girard, Nido R. Qubein, Roger Dawson, Les Hewitt, Bob Bloch, Mark Sanborn, and Joe Batten. Lee Shelton, especially, gave me a lot of encouragement.

Finally, I would like to express my gratitude to a few outstanding individuals who have greatly influenced my thinking. Like musicians who recognize the influence of previous artists on their careers, I would like to acknowledge the influence of these individuals on my thinking. They include Jim Rohn, Zig Ziglar, Larry Wingett, and especially the strategic coach Dan Sullivan. Through the ideas they shared in their books and audio recordings, they made a priceless contribution to my life.

There are many others who have helped. I am indebted to all of them.

About the Author

Andy J. Semotiuk has practiced law for more than 30 years. He is a member of the bar in the states of California and New York in the United States and in Ontario and British Columbia in Canada. In his work as an attorney, Semotiuk and has helped more than 10,000 clients, including thousands of young professionals, establish new roots as immigrants in the United States and Canada. During that time, Semotiuk served as Chairman of the Beverly Hills Bar Association Networking Committee for three years, where he advised young attorneys on establishing themselves in the legal profession. He has also mentored young people in professions like medicine, law, engineering, teaching, chiropractic, and psychology.

Semotiuk taught public speaking at the Ukrainian Catholic University in Lviv, Ukraine, in 2012 and earlier in the Faculty of Commerce at the University of British Columbia, in Vancouver, Canada. He has also given more than 3,000 presentations on various themes all over the world, as well as observing more than 5,000 presentations given by others. His public-speaking skills were further enhanced by doing stand-up comedy at the Pasadena Ice Palace and elsewhere in Los Angeles.

Prior to his career in law, Semotiuk worked as a United Nations correspondent stationed in New York. His articles were published by newspapers in the Southam newspaper chain in Canada as well as in various newspapers in the United States.

Other accomplishments include leading a campaign to raise over $2 million for a community college and running campaigns for candidates for national, regional, and local political offices.

Semotiuk lives in Toronto with his family and continues to practice immigration law with Pace Law Firm there and with Manning & Kass in Los Angeles.

Contents

Introduction

Trust life and it will teach you, in joy and sorrow, all you need to know.

–James Baldwin

When I first entered the legal profession as a young man, I was pretty green. As I matured in my legal career, however, I discovered that there was a cycle of learning involved in my profession. While I knew a lot about "the law," I knew very little about how things were done. Senior lawyers, secretaries, and paralegals taught me the practical things I now know. For example, it was a legal secretary who shared with me the need to always, always return a client's call in a timely fashion. Nothing drives home that point better than a frustrated legal secretary who has just dealt with a very angry client! In time, I learned the ropes. As we hired new staff, it became my role to teach these new people what I learned. This cycle has continued throughout my career and I respect it greatly. Many of the ideas I share in this book come from my involvement in this cycle of learning.

There are other professionals who could have written a book like this one, but few other professionals come into contact with as many young professionals from different countries as I do practicing immigration law in the United States and Canada. Even fewer are qualified to practice in four jurisdictions across the U.S. and Canada. I have worked in New York, Los Angeles, Toronto, and Edmonton to name just a few. This, I believe, gives me a unique perspective on life.

As an attorney over the past 30 years, I helped over 10,000 clients from various parts of the globe. My clients have included young professionals immigrating to the United States or Canada. By working with these individuals, I came to understand their hopes, dreams, and fears. Eventually, I came to realize that a book like this one might be helpful to them.

In my career, I noticed over and over again that colleagues in the legal community, as well as young people in other professions, had poor communication skills of even the most basic kind. I knew this was an area where I could certainly assist. With experience as a former teacher of public speaking in the Faculty of Commerce at the University of British Columbia, a member of Toastmasters International for more than 20 years, and a former United Nations correspondent, I felt I had sufficient credentials to help them. I presented my ideas to professional groups at various venues, including a national medical conference in Washington D.C. and the Barristers group of the Beverly Hills Bar Association in Los Angeles. However, it became clear that few people were ready to make the effort required to improve their communication skills. More than just presentations were needed. So I decided to write an article about what I knew on the subject.

Meanwhile, as Chairman of the Networking Committee of the Beverly Hills Bar Association from 2002 to 2005, I was often approached by young attorneys and other professionals just visiting us, eager to get my advice on how they could best succeed in their chosen professions. It was Kathy Johnston, a career counselor I admire very much, who first suggested I write a book specifically for young professionals. She pointed out that the marketplace was saturated with general self-help books, but there was a crying need for someone to address the challenges facing young attorneys. The same views were expressed by Dale and Peggy Howard, who both have PhD degrees in psychology. Dale Howard suggested the title of the book should be *The Young Professional*. And so the idea of this book was born.

I would like to make a few comments on the contents of the book and my life experience in general. No matter how long you live, you will not have enough time to learn everything there is to know. They say you learn best by making mistakes and drawing lessons from them. Because you are limited as to the number of experiences you can have in one lifetime, it only makes sense to seek to learn from others who were there before. The value of what you might learn from this book is that it is not based on untried academic theories.

Instead, the ideas I share here come from the practical world where I actually spent my career. I do not expect you to adopt every idea presented here, but I am hopeful there are at least some ideas you can put to use in your life right away.

The incredible diversity of people who came into my life during the course of my career is certainly a major theme of this book. Such diversity causes many people to reflect on their own heritage. Whether your background is Anglo-Celtic, Jewish, African, Asian, or Hispanic, you were born into a specific family and in some distinct place. These are matters over which you had no control. Yet, they do influence your life. Certainly my life was shaped, at least in part, by my background, as you will see from some of the stories included in this book.

In my case, my family immigrated to the United States and Canada from Ukraine. I was born in Western Canada and lived there as well as later on in Los Angeles. Even while living in the U.S., I have maintained strong ties to my Ukrainian-Canadian heritage. Through it, I was privileged to meet some extraordinary Ukrainian individuals whose unique experiences are recounted in this book. Through learning about their experiences—both triumphs and failures—I was inspired and was taught invaluable life skills. It is my hope that their stories will affect you in the same way.

Ultimately, this book is about how you can be more successful in your career and happier in your life. When I use the word "success," I include things like making more money, being healthier, having a happier family, and finding spiritual contentment. But the best definition of success I have found was the one provided by Cavett Robert, the founder of the National Speakers Association. Cavett defined success as the progressive realization of meaningful goals. I like this definition because it focuses on the fact that success is a journey, not just a destination. Being successful, according to this view, implies making the best choices possible in all aspects of everyday life. When all is said and done, that is what this book is designed to help you achieve.

Andy J. Semotiuk

Just a Quick Snooze Can Get You in Trouble

Some time ago, I decided to go to a movie. When I arrived at the theater in Pasadena, I learned that the show didn't start until eight. Since it was only six o'clock, I had about two hours to kill. As I thought about what to do, I realized I was tired. I decided to drive down to the nearby Rose Bowl parking area, where I could rest while sitting in my car. "Maybe," I thought to myself, "I can get a few moments of shut-eye."

As I sat there, however, I was constantly disturbed by cars driving back and forth, kids shouting, people learning how to drive, and picnickers. It soon became clear to me that I would not be getting any rest if I stayed here. I decided to move. But where?

As I drove down the road, I came to an empty field under a bridge. It seemed quiet enough. Although it was fenced in, the gate was wide open and nobody was around. I decided to park there and soon fell asleep. When I woke up, it was dark. I looked at my watch and realized it was 7:45 p.m. "Just in time to make it to the movie," I thought. Then I looked up. Someone had locked the main gate.

At first, I was astonished. I couldn't believe it! How could anyone come along and close this gate without seeing me in my car? Then I became angry. Who was the idiot who locked me in here? Then I thought, "Wait a minute. *I'm* the idiot. I'm the one parked in somebody else's lot."

I surveyed the yard in the hopes of finding another exit. None seemed evident.

"Surely they have other gates," I thought. "I'll drive around the perimeter of the area and check." Like a crazed animal locked in a cage, I drove up and down the yard in search of another gate. There was none. I was locked in for the night.

My frustration and anxiety gave way to despair. The thought of having to explain why my car was locked in somebody else's yard filled me with humiliation. Years of positive thinking went right out the window as I sank down in disgust with myself for being so stupid. Hey, I'm hard on myself in times like these!

In the distance I could see lights inside a building. Judging by the military vehicles in the lot, I surmised the building had to be some sort of army installation. Was there room for hope? I devised a plan to attract the attention of somebody in that building without annoying the neighbors living in houses around the area. I decided to blow my car horn, but only intermittently. Genius at work! But, no luck. "I'd better stop before I really irritate someone," I thought. But what could I do?

It became clear I had to climb the fence to find someone who could open the gate. As I looked up, I noticed barbed wire on top. I decided to scale it anyway. The barbed wire did its job. I cut my hand and tore a hole in my best pair of pants. There was just no way I was going to get over that fence. I drove my car to another spot where there was no barbed wire. I parked close to the fence so I could use the car to get over the fence. I almost killed myself, but I made it! As Winston Churchill put it, "In the face of defeat, defiance!"

I walked over to the military building. A large sign announced, "Military Reserve Headquarters." I peered inside the windows and knocked on the doors. No response. I knew buildings like these normally have a night bell, but for the life of me I could not find one. I stepped back from the building to survey what else I could do.

As I looked at the front of the building in the darkness, I noticed a huge red arrow painted on the front. I'm talking like 10 feet high. I wondered what the arrow was for. As I looked more carefully, I saw a button— the night bell! I rang it. Again and again. No answer! I felt crushed. Saturday night, and nobody was around. What do I do now?

I looked around. Across the street, I saw a house with the lights on. Some guy was working on his computer. I decided to ask him to call the army to open the gate. Luckily, he opened the door, believed my story, and let me make my phone call. But try calling any government office at eight o'clock on Saturday night. Ha! Short of calling someone in the Pentagon in Washington, D.C., you're not going to reach anyone. As far as the military is concerned, help yourself to whatever you want; just turn the lights off before you leave. I sank down on the man's couch in resignation.

"Okay, can you please just call me a cab?" I asked him.

The next morning when I returned, the gate was open. I got in my car and drove off.

When I first thought about sharing this story publicly, I hesitated. After all, it just proves what a fool I can be. But the more I thought about it, the more I realized that the experience was really a miniature metaphor of my life's journey. When I think about it, I feel like a person who remembers a snowy night while looking into one of those glass souvenirs in a gift store that, when tipped upside down, portrays a melancholy winter scene. Except when I reflect on *this* experience, it evokes not just one, but a whole range of emotions in me. That is why the story is so powerful. Experiencing emotions, even when they are not positive, is one of the most meaningful and unique aspects of being human. While your life's medley may be interrupted by a false note from time to time, like my life was in this experience, the trick is to make the best of a bad situation. The underlying message in this story is that instead of lamenting the false note, you have to finish the symphony. That is the main message in this book.

In this book, I have recounted many stories like this one from my life, both positive and negative. By sharing them, I hope to make it easier for you to tackle the problems that no doubt will confront you in your career. My hope is that in these pages you will find inspiration and some practical guidance to help you enjoy your achievements and overcome any setbacks ahead.

DARE TO BE UNIQUE

Real success is finding your lifework in the work that you love.

—David McCullough

I enjoy a great variety of music—especially hits from the past. One of my favorite singers from the era of rock and roll was Elvis Presley. I particularly liked songs from the latter part of his career, like "Love Me Tender," "Wooden Heart," and "Love Letters."

Elvis's music touched me and inspired me to read some of his biographies. One thing about his life struck me as particularly interesting: He never really lived until he performed on stage. It was on center stage entertaining audiences that he felt most comfortable, most at home, and most alive.

This phenomenon is sometimes referred to as the "Wallenda Effect," named after Karl Wallenda, a famous tightrope walker who achieved world fame for his acrobatic abilities, and who ultimately met his death in San Juan, Puerto Rico, in 1978. His wife told reporters in later interviews that for Wallenda, life was lived entertaining audiences while on the high wire. He felt like a dead man on the ground. Wallenda put it this way: All his life was either a prelude to or a footnote after entertaining audiences while walking the tightrope.

The circumstances that create the Wallenda Effect were studied by Mihaly Csikszentmihalyi, a professor of psychology at Claremont Graduate University in Claremont, California. Csikszentmihalyi discusses the concept of "flow," which is a person's state when that person is enjoying what he or she is doing and is so focused on the activity that the person submerges his or her self-consciousness into the moment. Csikszentmihalyi describes this state as one of intense concentration—a laser-like focus in which time passes unnoticed.

5

For example, one might emerge from the activity and find that what may have seemed like five minutes was actually two hours.

This concept of being on center stage, this Wallenda Effect, this idea of flow, is intriguing. Another way of looking at it is through the "Table of Abilities," a concept introduced by Dan Sullivan, a strategic coach who lives in Toronto, Canada. His concept has had a revolutionary impact on my life.

Imagine a chart in front of you, a table with a horizontal line on the top—a place to write or type your name. Now imagine that at this moment, you are writing or typing your name on the top of the chart. See yourself writing in your name. This chart is now your chart, and it will portray your life skills and abilities.

Now suppose that you have come across a fantastic new computer that has just analyzed your entire life history, with input from all your friends and relatives, concerning your skills and abilities. Imagine this computer filling a column down the left side of the table with each and every skill and ability that you possess. This might include abilities such as making a peanut butter and jelly sandwich, riding a bicycle, reading a book, composing a poem, or doing complex brain surgery. Imagine further that the same computer has also sorted your abilities into four columns across the page, labeled "Incompetent," "Competent," "Excellent," and "Unique."

If the computer ranked each one of your abilities and skills into one of these four columns, at the end of the exercise, about 95 percent of your abilities would fall into the Competent or Excellent category. Very few might fall into the Incompetent column, and a few abilities might fall into the Unique column. In my case, for example, a computer might rank my skills as follows:

- ✢ **Making peanut butter and jelly sandwiches:** Competent
- ✢ **Reading:** Competent
- ✢ **Writing:** Excellent
- ✢ **Speaking:** Excellent

Then it might come to a skill like assembling anything newly purchased that comes in a box. This would end up in the Incompetent column. I can *do* assembly, but, let's face it: I'm just not competent at it.

The world knows it, and I know it. Frankly, my blood pressure starts rising as soon as I start thinking about it. The reality is that I am better off leaving this activity to someone else.

There are a few skills and abilities that each one of us has that fall in the Incompetent category, but this is no reason for alarm. Will Rogers once said, "We are all ignorant, except in different areas." He was right. But what is more important is the other column: the Unique column, which reveals the skills you have that may put you on center stage, into the Wallenda Effect, into flow.

You can identify your unique abilities by asking yourself what you find easy and enjoyable. Perhaps it is an activity you enjoyed in childhood, or maybe it is something that completely absorbs you. What are you better at than anyone else? Not every ability will be a useful one. You might be unique in your ability to play tiddlywinks, but this may not be something in high demand. The key is to find an ability that is needed out there in the world, and one for which you have a passion.

Let me illustrate how I used this philosophy with an example from my own career. When I moved to Los Angeles and looked for legal work, I soon realized that the market here was extremely competitive. I was forced to analyze myself and my career to look for abilities I could market in Los Angeles. Going through my table of abilities, I realized that I have one unique trait that, as far as I know, no other attorney has: I am the only licensed Canadian immigration attorney practicing in Los Angeles. No other attorney is licensed to do Canadian, as well as U.S., immigration law in L.A. I'm the only one. I don't have to chase after ambulances for clients. I don't have to put up billboards saying, "Need a Lawyer? Call: 555-5555." By definition, because my ability is unique, I have a monopoly. There is no one to compete with.

I am convinced that the key to success in your career, and indeed in your life, really boils down to this one idea. As the best-selling author of *Shut Up, Stop Whining & Get A Life* Larry Wingett points out, the challenge is to "discover your uniqueness and learn to exploit it in the service of others and you will be guaranteed success, happiness and prosperity."

LIVING A HEALTHY LIFESTYLE

Health is by far the most important element in human happiness.

—Arthur Schopenhauer (1851)

A man went to see his doctor.
He declared, "I am planning to live forever."
The doctor said, "I see. So how is it going?"
The man said, "So far...so good."

Your health is one of the most important aspects of your life. Whenever I see people abusing their health, I see red—but not because I get angry. No, I see RED—an acronym that represents good health. R stands for rest, E stands for exercise, and D stands for diet. Over the years, I have studied these areas very carefully. Here is what I have come up with so far. Some of this will be familiar to you, but it never hurts to review the basics.

Rest

The first basic of good health is rest. Start with about eight hours of sleep a night. Eight hours is a rough number, and your body will tell you whether that's enough. You may need as much as nine hours, or perhaps as little as seven. As you grow older, you tend not to need as much sleep. But, on average, you need eight hours of sleep a night.

They say that the hours of sleep before midnight are the most important hours of your nightly rest because that is when you get your deepest sleep. As the saying goes, "Early to bed, early to rise, makes a man healthy, wealthy, and wise."

Because you spend so much of your life sleeping, what you sleep on is incredibly important. Indeed, you spend virtually half your life on your bed, so make sure to have a good one. Don't scrimp on this. Also make sure your bedroom is comfortable and conducive to a good night's sleep.

Some executives find it helpful to take a short nap during the middle of their workday. President John F. Kennedy and British Prime Minister Winston Churchill, among other leaders, used to follow this practice. I found it very helpful, particularly when my children were small and I didn't always get a full night's sleep. About 15 or 20 minutes of rest was usually more than enough to keep me going.

Rest also entails the notion of vacations. Everyone needs to take a vacation once in a while. Failing to take a vacation is like driving a car without changing the oil. Ultimately, it can lead to a disaster. Your body sends signals indicating that it's time for a vacation. It might be a migraine headache, tension in your back, or an ulcer. If you keep denying these signals because you don't have time, you are too busy, or for some other reason, your body is going to take a vacation whether you like it or not. That's when you end up in the hospital.

I don't know how it is in your life, but in my life, I always have a thousand reasons why I can't take a vacation. I can't afford one. I don't have time for one. And I am always too busy to take one. But, I have learned that I need to take vacations, whether I like it or not. Moreover, when I do, I am always glad that I did. As Dan Sullivan, the Canadian strategic coach and business adviser, points out, there is a positive correlation (within reason) between how much vacation time senior executives take and their productivity at work.

In addition to standing for the word rest, the letter R also stands for the word reflection. At the end of every day, take time to review and ask yourself, what was your best achievement today? What did you learn? Who came into your life that you were thankful for?

Ask similar questions at the end of every week. From time to time—perhaps monthly or quarterly—look back at the last stretch and ask similar questions again. And at the end of the year, reflect on your year's achievements and what you are proud of. Consider how your life is developing with respect to your mission, values, and goals. Ask yourself how you can do better.

So, there you are: rest and reflection, the first part of a three-part health program.

Exercise

After driving all night, a man pulled over in a park to get some rest. Just as he was dozing off, he was awakened by a knock on the window. "What time is it?" asked a jogger. "7:30," answered the man drowsily. Just as he dozed off again, another jogger knocked on his window. "What time is it?" asked the jogger. "7:45," answered the man. Again, he tried to sleep, only to be awakened by another jogger asking the same question. That was the last straw. After answering the jogger, the man put a sign in his window saying "I don't know the time!" Just as he fell asleep, another jogger pounded on his window and shouted, "Hey, buddy, it's 7:55!"

That's a story about persistence. And when it comes to exercise, I believe you have to be persistent—to exercise every working day without exception. I say "working day" because most people have a five-day work week. They say five days of exercise per week is the minimum recommended amount.

Of all the three elements of a healthy lifestyle—rest, exercise, and diet—most people find exercise to be the hardest. It is difficult to maintain a long-term steady regimen of exercise. Because it's hard, I find that the best time to exercise is first thing in the morning. (This is probably the most important point I make in this book as far as leading a healthy lifestyle is concerned.) Later in the day, things tend to creep up on you—things that you did not expect earlier in the day. They crowd out your intention to exercise. Someone dies and there is a funeral, someone just flew into town, a meeting is extended longer than you thought, your car has developed some kind of problem, you forgot it's your turn to take the kids to lessons, and a hundred other excuses lie in wait for you if you do not exercise first thing in the morning. I believe it takes twice the discipline to exercise at any other time of the day as it does in the morning. As difficult as it may be to wake yourself up early enough to exercise before you get into your daily routine, you just have to do it. "Mind over mattress," as Steven Covey would say.

That said, it is better to exercise any time of the day than not at all. If you're not a morning person, I suggest you try to become a morning person. But if you just can't do it, then it is better for you to do some exercise, no matter what time of day, than no exercise at all. (By the way, I'm not a morning person either, but life's demands taught me to become a morning person.)

In my opinion, the key to a good workout is, at the very least, to break a sweat. That means some sort of aerobic exercise—running, jogging, bicycling, swimming…it really doesn't matter, as long as you break a sweat. But breaking a sweat is not everything, and it's probably not enough. Recent health reports indicate that the best sort of exercise is strenuous exercise, such as playing tennis or racquetball. Games like golf, or walking outdoors—while better than nothing—are not nearly as good as a competitive sport. But, one good thing that golf has over other forms of exercise is fresh air, and one cannot overestimate the importance of fresh air!

If you're interested in losing weight, according to the experts, a key consideration is that weight loss begins after the first 30 minutes of exercise. I found in my own experience that when I exercised for more than 30 minutes, every extra minute longer resulted in pounds just dropping off.

Diet

When I was young, my aging uncle used to tell me I could eat broken glass and bent nails and it won't have any effect on me now, but wait until I turned 30! Well he was wrong—it happened when I turned 31. My metabolism changed completely. I realized he was right. The older I get, the more concerned I am about my diet in particular and my health in general.

The starting point with respect to diet is to eat breakfast like a king, lunch like a prince, supper like a pauper, and no snacks. A variation on this is to eat small meals five times a day rather than three large meals. The most important thing is not to eat late at night. The earlier you eat, the better.

By the way, if you *do* want to be fat, don't bother to eat breakfast. That way, you can starve your system and build up a big appetite for bingeing later. Also, if fat is what you're after, eat lots of pasta, pizza, Chinese food (which has a lot of oil), processed foods, white bread, and rice. Buy fatty products, like bacon, and use lots of butter. Eat a lot of fried foods, especially French fries and fried chicken. Add a lot of ice cream, candies, chips, chocolate bars, creamy soups, sauces, and fillings. At receptions in the business world, keep nibbling on *hors d'oeuvres* before your meal arrives. Also, drink a lot of soft drinks and make sure you don't drink any water. That way, the sludge in your bloodstream can clog your liver and kidneys and build up an excess of toxins in your body.

If you want to die early, here is an easy way to do that: Consume a lot of sugar, salt, and white flour. Sugar will add on the calories that can contribute to diabetes and other illnesses. Salt will lead to high blood pressure and strokes. White flour will lead to high cholesterol and, ultimately, to heart attacks. And, by all means, keep consuming large quantities of alcohol and coffee, and top them off with a few smokes every day.

I think you get the message. Look, nobody is perfect. I'm sure not. But we have to do the best we can. In the end, you are what you eat, so eat healthy.

Conclusion

In each of these areas, there are things you can do to improve. For example, you can get a good bed to rest better, join a travel club to plan vacations, join the YMCA for exercise, or join Weight Watchers for diet. The only critical element in all this is, what direction are you headed? It doesn't matter whether you run a mile a day (or even 15 miles), or whether you eat healthy or you eat French fries at every meal.

The key element is simply the direction you're going. As long as you're going in the right direction in each of these three areas, that is all you can ask of yourself. In time, incremental, marginal improvements on a daily basis will result in a healthy lifestyle. To draw an analogy, you don't have to demolish an old house and then start from scratch. You can replace one nail and one board at a time. If you do just that, in time, you will have a completely renovated modern house. The same is true for your body.

COMMON COURTESY

The small courtesies sweeten life; the greater, ennoble it.

–Minnesota proverb

In 1972, while I was studying for my law exams in Vancouver, Canada, my good friend John Kolasky came to me to ask me a very important question. I could tell it was important to him by the look in his eyes and the way he approached me.

He asked, "Andy, does the end justify the means?" Or, as he put it another way, "Can you achieve a higher goal by doing something evil?" An elderly, delicate, balding man, Kolasky searched my face to see if I could come up with an intelligent response.

Back then, I was pretty young, and I didn't have a good answer to such an important question. So I leaned back and shrugged my shoulders. Kolasky proceeded to lecture me while I willingly absorbed what he said. He said that each means you choose is in fact an end in itself. It is impossible to choose a bad means and have it result in a good end. This was a profound moral insight both for me and for him.

The insight was that you have to take a morally acceptable approach in everything you do. It meant that you have to treat every person as an end, not just as a means to your end. It meant that it is wrong to employ coercion with or violence against others; you have to deal with each person by agreement or not at all. It meant that the state cannot sacrifice the individual for the sake of achieving some higher goal. But it also meant that when the only choices are the life of one person and the life of everyone on an airplane, for example, then it is proper to kill one person if it will save the lives of everyone else.

This thinking has an application in the area of the professional practice. The moral question can be put as follows: Can you use someone to get ahead in your career? The answer is no...unless that person agrees to help you in getting ahead.

A simple example in the office context is giving someone your undivided attention. Sometimes, when someone comes to your office to speak to you, you may have a number of things going on. The phone may be ringing, you may be composing an email, etc. Of course, if the person is interrupting you in the midst of something important, you must ask him or her to come back on another occasion. But if you're prepared to speak with the person, it's important to give him or her your undivided attention. That means you need to block calls for the period of time that you're talking to him or her. It also means that you need to prevent other people from entering or interrupting your discussion. Don't just take the conversation at face value. You also need to be alert to pick up the unspoken message in the conversation. Sometimes what is troubling a visitor is not readily apparent. It may be two or three questions deep. Ask those probing questions. If you're going to talk to someone, give that person your honest, undivided attention.

Another way of stating the same point is to say that all people merit your full attention, whether they are weak or powerful. You should treat each the same. A waiter, a barber, or a bus driver are all entitled to the same respect from you that the president of the United States would get. We have a natural human tendency to ingratiate ourselves, sometimes shamelessly, with powerful people who we deal with. Although I know better, I sometimes catch myself trying to warm up to someone important at meetings or receptions at the expense of those in front of me. Then I wonder what has come over me. It's important to resist this propensity.

In the early 1980s, I used to carpool to work with a friend of mine, Alex Brodsky, who came to Canada from the Soviet Union. Every morning, Alex would come to my house and pick me up, and we would ride in his car to work downtown. While riding one day, Alex pointed out an element of courtesy that he had noticed: Often, the people he met at work avoided him or avoided eye contact while they were passing by in the corridors. But where he grew up, he was taught that it was common courtesy to say, "Good morning!" Whether you liked the person, whether you got along, was not important. Saying "good morning" in these circumstances was simply an acknowledgment of another person's humanity.

Many years later, after I passed the California State Bar exam and started working for a law firm, I came to better appreciate Alex's comments. Each morning, as I passed people with whom I worked, I noticed that they passed by without acknowledging me. Often, they attended busily to their work, avoiding eye contact. So I began making it a point every day to say, "Good morning!" to each one of them by name. I know this irritated them, but they would reluctantly reply, "Good morning, Andy." Over time, I wore them down. Now, whenever I see them, they say "good morning" and sometimes even add a smile. It's only common courtesy.

One of the most elementary courtesies you can extend to a person with whom you are speaking for some period of time is to either stand up to speak with him or her, or invite him or her to sit down to speak with you. This is particularly important with older people. Similarly, when the phone rings in my office, I answer, "Andy Semotiuk speaking." I do this because I know most people have a difficult time pronouncing my name. I encourage you to do the same, particularly if you also have a difficult name to pronounce. Again, it is elementary courtesy.

In short, common courtesy requires that you treat other people the way you would want them to treat you. Treat people respectfully, no matter what their station in life. Be polite. Don't talk about people behind their backs. Exhibit good manners at all times. Never resort to profanity or inappropriate comments or behavior on the job or in any public setting. Whenever possible, be flexible and do things the way other people want them done (as long as you do not compromise yourself in the process).

When I was a youngster, my mother and father used to take me to a fast-food restaurant at the end of every school year to celebrate my success. Every time, my mother would pick up the garbage after we finished eating and put it away in the garbage bin. It drove me crazy!

I thought that that was the waitress's job. Now, however, I realize my mother was only showing common courtesy. These days, I pick up the garbage after I eat at a fast-food restaurant and make a point of trying to put away the tray in some suitable place. Similarly, when I leave a room, I make it a point to turn out the lights. To exhibit such courtesy is a part of being a noble human being and of respecting our environment.

You may be thinking, "This guy Semotiuk is lecturing me on the basics of life. I already know this stuff!" But a reminder never hurts. By practicing these little disciplines, we build a better character all around. Neglect in one area tends to build neglect in others. Try to always extend every courtesy to everyone around you.

THE ROAD TO A MORE
POSITIVE PERSPECTIVE
AND A HAPPIER LIFE

Happiness is not achieved by the conscious pursuit of happiness;
it is generally the by-product of other activities.

–Aldous Huxley (1945)

"It is important to come to grips with the reality that problems are an integral, ongoing part of the living experience," says Robert Ringer in his book, *Million Dollar Habits*. "Life is a never-ending stream of hardships, obstacles, rejection, frustrations, and so-called bad luck. Life is lost jobs, loans that aren't granted, sales that don't close, people who treat us unfairly, and deals that fall through at the last minute. None of these are fatal; they're just life."

Keeping your affairs in perspective can sometimes be a matter of life and death. A good illustration of this fact was an experience I had in the early 1970s near Creston, British Columbia, in the Canadian Rockies. Back then, I was a student living in Toronto. I was to deliver a truck to Vancouver for a shipping agent back east. He paid for the gas, and I drove the truck. My plan was to make my way to Vancouver and then down to Los Angeles, where my family was gathering for Christmas.

I started out in Toronto. When I reached Sudbury, in Northern Ontario, I developed some engine problems, and stopped at a service station. For some fortuitous reason, a stroke of luck, I happened to pick the station where this same truck had been serviced previously by one of the mechanics. He told me that this truck had been totaled and that there was a problem with the carburetor. He taught me how to fix the truck when it stalled. He showed me how to take off the air filter and pour a little gasoline into the carburetor to get the truck started again.

I didn't have any further problems with the truck after that. The mechanic had evidently fixed what was wrong and I knew what to do if I had trouble. It was fine all the way from Sudbury to Creston. Outside Creston is a mountain where the highway travels straight uphill for 13 miles. This is one of the highest points in North America. It was late, around midnight, so there wasn't much traffic. I was virtually alone on the highway.

When I reached the foot of that summit drive, I noticed that it was snowing lightly. As I started up the incline, I noticed the snow getting heavier. About five miles later, the highway was completely covered in snow. It was becoming very difficult for the truck to make its way up the road. I passed a sign that said "Avalanche Area Next 5 Miles." A few miles further ahead, my tires began spinning. I slowed down from an initial speed of 65 miles per hour to about 35. By the 11-mile mark, I was down to about 10 miles an hour. And by the 12-mile mark, I was having trouble controlling the truck. It was dancing all over the slick road. I was down to 5 miles per hour. To my right was a huge mountain, straight up. To my left was a huge precipice, straight down. It was dark. There were no other cars traveling in either direction.

I began to worry that I wouldn't make it to the top. Sure enough, about half a mile further up the road, my truck spun out of control. Luckily, I ended up stuck on the right side of the road. My two right tires embedded themselves into a ditch. My truck also conked out. There I was, in complete darkness. The snow was heavy, and there was a slick sheet of ice beneath me. There was no other traffic on the highway. It was freezing cold outside, and there was no heat inside. There was a huge mountain on my right side, there was a huge abyss on my left, and I was stuck!

I tried to start the truck. The engine turned over, but it didn't catch. I tried again. It wouldn't start. I recalled the mechanic's advice in Sudbury. I got out, opened the hood, and took off the air filter. I poured some gas into the carburetor. I got back into the truck, and

I turned the key yet again. Luckily, the engine started. Partial relief! At least I wasn't going to freeze to death. By now, the road was completely covered in snow. I closed the hood, put everything away, and got back into the truck. Now I had to figure out how to get out of this ditch. I tried moving forward and then backward, but it was futile. I was stuck.

Then I saw the lights of another vehicle over the horizon. He was coming down the road in my direction. Suddenly, I was gripped with fear. As the car traveled toward me, I imagined that the driver would panic when he saw me, lose control, and either crash into my vehicle or go straight over the edge into the abyss. I hit my horn. I leaned on it. The other vehicle turned out to be a small truck. Fortunately, the driver was smart enough to be traveling at a very slow speed. He managed to slow down when he saw my lights. He put on his brakes, slid for probably 200 yards, and finally stopped about 10 feet away from me and got out.

He was a cowboy, wearing a cowboy hat. He said, "Obviously, you got trouble."

I said, "Yeah, could you help me get out of the ditch? I'm stuck!"

"Sure. How did you end up on this road?"

"Well, I was just on my way to Vancouver," I replied.

"Did you know that the road is closed?"

"No."

He said he was the last truck allowed to go on the summit because of the snow and the possibility of an avalanche. "Hop in your truck and I'll pull out this chain and see if I can pull you out of the ditch there." So, while I sat, he connected the chain to the back of his truck and then to the back of my truck, pulling my truck backward down to the road. He managed to pull my back end out of the ditch first, and then my front end followed. I ended up facing uphill on the road, my engine running, out of the ditch. He got out of his truck and asked me if I thought I'd be okay. I said yes. I sensed he was anxious to be on his way. He then put the chain back in his truck and drove off.

So, there I was, sitting on the highway, and I had to make a decision. Should I try to make it to the top of the summit, or should I turn around and go the other way? One of the concerns that crossed my mind was whether another vehicle might come over that crest and collide with me as I tried to turn around on this slippery sheet of ice. But, after weighing the alternatives, I decided I might as well turn around. My truck just was not going to make it over the crest. Somehow, I managed to stay out of the ditch.

I started driving back down to Creston. Again, I passed a sign that said "Avalanche Area Next 5 Miles." I knew I was one of the last vehicles on the highway driving toward Creston. I started praying that there would be no avalanches as I drove those five miles. The road was very slippery. I could go out of control if I went too fast. If I went out of control, I would go over the cliff and that would be the end of me. Yet, I wanted to get out of the avalanche area as quickly as possible. These two factors weighed in my mind as I drove down that highway late that night.

As I drove the last mile or so, it seemed to me that I heard a rumbling sound, as though behind me there was an avalanche coming down. I drove as fast as I could without losing control. I distinctly remember shouting "Come on, baby!" to the truck as I drove faster and faster down the road. Somehow, thankfully, I made it! Back down in Creston, as I came to the foot of the mountain, there was a police car blocking the road with its lights flashing. The policeman stopped me.

"Where did you come from?"

"Well," I said, "I was up on the hill."

"Did you realize that there was an avalanche up on that mountain?"

"No."

"Were there any other cars behind you?"

"No, I was the only one up there. I got stuck in a ditch and one of the other drivers helped me get out."

"You should thank your lucky stars for getting off that mountain before that avalanche hit!"

So, I made my way back to Creston, and from there I took an alternate route to Vancouver. I then hopped on a plane and got to Los Angeles on Christmas Eve, just in time for dinner with my family.

That experience shows how important a proper perspective can be to our survival in life. That night, on the mountain, instead of finding solutions to my dilemma, I could have concentrated on my fears. In large measure, life is a self-fulfilling prophecy. You get what you are looking for. If I had allowed myself to dwell on my fears of freezing to death, slipping over the edge, or crashing into oncoming traffic, that is what could have happened. My perspective would have disarmed me. Luckily, however, I kept my fears in their proper perspective, which empowered me to act in a manner that resolved the crisis. The key is to remember that no matter what the circumstances, you alone are in control of your perspective.

For me, the best illustration of how to keep your life in perspective was in the book *How To Stop Worrying and Start Living* by Dale Carnegie. In that book, Carnegie invites us to imagine our lives, including everything we know and everything we have touched, as a large circle drawn on a piece of paper. He then asks us to imagine a black dot drawn in the center of the circle. Carnegie explains that the black dot represents the problems we are facing at the moment. He says that no matter how grave your problems are, they really are only a small part of the larger circle of your life. However, he adds, if you focus just on the black dot (your problems) without keeping it in perspective, it will grow relative to the larger circle (representing your life). It is a matter of how you frame your problems in your mind.

A Matter of Perspective

Two boys were playing basketball. Suddenly a vicious dog attacked one of them. The other found a stick and beat the dog away. A sports reporter saw everything. He pulled out his notebook and wrote, "Brave Dodgers Fan Saves Friend from Vicious Dog."

"But," the boy said, "I'm not a Dodgers fan."

"Oh," said the reporter, "I assumed you were, since we are in L.A. So who do you cheer for?"

The boy answered, "I'm a Giants fan."

The reporter turned the page in his notebook and wrote, "Little Hooligan from San Francisco Almost Kills Family Pet!"

How to Find Focus and Meaning in Your Life

*Obstacles are those frightful things you see when
you take your eyes off your goal.*

–Henry Ford

In a way, living your life is like holding a pencil in your hand. Your hand directs the pencil just as your willpower directs what you do in life. To write effectively, your pencil must be sharp. To be effective in your life, your mind must be focused. As you use a pencil, it becomes dull. You have to re-sharpen it from time to time. The same is true of focus. As you go through life, turbulence hits you. You lose your focus. Your focus becomes blurred. You have to re-sharpen your focus the way you re-sharpen your pencil.

As I was thinking about focus in life, the analogy of a pencil was especially valuable because you can only use a pencil so long before it reaches the end. Life is like that—we are only here for a time. You can spend all your life sharpening your focus. However, I hope that is not all you are doing. The idea is not just to have a sharp pencil, but to use it. Similarly, in life, the idea is not just to have a sharp focus, but to use it for achieving the goals. On the other hand, you can have a pencil that's too sharp—so sharp that as soon as you begin to write with it, the lead breaks. The same is true of focus. If you spend your whole life planning every little detail of everything you are going to do, your plans will fall apart as soon as they come into contact with the reality of life. So, the idea is to have a useable, working focus—a pencil that is sharp, as well as useable.

The cruise missile is one of the most sophisticated missiles ever created. It provides another useful analogy in looking at the need for focus. The cruise missile is computer-guided. The missile pursues its target through a computer program that tells the missile in advance how to fly over the terrain. Because of this low-flying capability, the cruise missile is very hard to detect. Through its computer program, it knows when to climb over mountains and when to descend into valleys. As with the cruise missile, so it is with our life. You need a target to shoot for, to aim at. If you don't have such a target, at some point you run out of gas and you fizzle out. If you don't have a target, you are going to burn out. There is a lot of pressure in life to shoot, shoot, shoot! But, there is very little concern over the question, "Shoot at what?" It is shooting at the right target that counts. Focus relates to spending time looking for the target in your life—for that unique ability you have that you can offer the world.

Focus Involves Three Components

I think there are three areas that you have to explore to find focus and maybe some of the meaning in your life. They are as follows:

- A personal mission statement
- Values
- Goals

A Personal Mission Statement

At some point in life, you might feel like asking yourself these questions:

- "Why am I here on this Earth?"
- "Why was I put here?"
- "What am I supposed to contribute to this world?"

A personal mission statement answers these questions. It is a concise expression of the purpose of your life. This is not something you figure out over a sip of coffee or by sitting down for a minute to write down some ideas. This is something that takes a long time and a lot of effort. The answers that you ultimately come up with will define your mission statement. My philosophy is that every person needs a mission statement.

Finding and expressing your mission statement is one of the biggest challenges of your life. Here's a rule that I follow, and I believe it can be very useful to you, too. I picked it up from Robert Townsend, one of the leading business commentators in the United States. He says that you don't have a mission statement unless it can be expressed in seven words or less. Let me repeat: in seven words or less! Now, I know that is a big challenge, but it has to be done because only then does it become crystal clear and easy to remember.

My experiences in preparing a résumé and a personal brochure helped me sort out my mission statement. While working on my résumé, I always searched for a broader definition of my purpose in life. Then, an important event propelled me even further down the road of self-definition: a meeting I had with Greg Korneluk at a National Speakers' Association conference. Greg took me off to one side and showed me a brochure that he had prepared about himself. Frankly, it was the best brochure I had ever seen. He had collected some of the best brochures that other people had prepared and made it a point to make his even better than the best.

By seeing the best available, I knew what standard I would have to attain. I decided right then and there that I, too, would prepare a brochure about myself. I would include recommendations from my clients, as well as pictures from my life. I decided to do a write-up of what I had done in more depth and detail than the brochures I had prepared up until that time. It's been a few years since then; today, instead of brochures, we use websites. But I still strive to meet the same standard of excellence on the Internet.

I don't think my mission statement is perfect, but it is as far as I have gone in expressing my own purpose in life. So I would like to share it with you:

Sharing meaningful experiences with significant others.

It is a work in progress, but it has helped me greatly.

Values

I find the best way to deal with the subject of values is to use the analogy of mining for gold. To be successful in gold mining, you have to know not only how to dig for gold, but also where to dig! When digging for gold, you have to move a tremendous amount of soil to find a few valuable nuggets. Life is like that, too. There are all kinds of administrative and logistical things that we have to handle while enjoying life. As we move this "soil" out of the way, we must be on the lookout for the valuable nuggets that life has to offer us. In digging for gold in life, what we are really digging for are values. To find the values in life, we must explore deep inside ourselves. There is an entire universe inside each one of us, waiting to be explored. You could spend your whole life just exploring this universe between your ears.

In my own life I've identified five key values that I think are very important to lead a successful life and find happiness. I am not saying that these are the only values or that they have to be your values, but I am going to offer them to you as values that you should consider. A whole discussion could be undertaken on each one of these values, but here I have tried to express the key points of each. They are as follows:

❖ **Integrity.** Integrity is listening to the internal voice that tells you what is right or wrong, and then doing the right thing. Also, it is being honest with ourselves and others, even when it's uncomfortable to do so.

❖ **Courage.** Courage is similar to integrity. In fact, when I discussed this with my wife, she suggested that integrity and courage were really the same thing. But as we talked about it more, we came up with a distinction. You see, you have to have courage to have integrity, but not vice versa. You can be evil and still have courage. Courage, as I understand it, is that quality that makes you face the challenges in your life the way you want to face them or the way you *should* face them. It is doing the things that you feel are right even when other people think that those things are wrong.

❖ **Tenacity.** Tenacity means sticking to something you believe in, right to the end. I think the best way to describe tenacity is to say that it is the quality that makes you stick to something long after your initial enthusiasm for it has dimmed, until that task is complete.

✣ **Loyalty.** Although this quality is much maligned these days, it is one that you should show in your relationships—not only to your family members, but also to your boss or employees. Loyalty is what causes you to reciprocate to the people who show goodwill to you by showing goodwill back to them to the same degree or, perhaps, even more.

✣ **Balance.** Balance means keeping everything in perspective. It requires a "total systems" approach to life, not sacrificing one part of your life for the sake of another.

As time passes, I find my values changing. For example, since I first wrote this passage a few years ago, new values have emerged in my life. Values like honesty, sincerity, love, and compassion have taken on more prominence. I know the same is true for others.

There is, of course, no shortage of values you can choose from. The point is to explore values like these to determine which ones are your key values. This will help you to get a better grip on where you are going in your life. And that brings us to the subject of goals.

Goals

In seeking to clarify your focus, you should also look at your goals. Again, this is a topic in itself. I believe that developing a mission statement and sorting out your values comes before setting good goals. Briefly, I would say goals are something we need for the long term, the short term, and each day. Jim Rohn's approach to setting goals was the best I have seen. Jim was considered America's Business Philosopher and leading trainer until his death in December of 2009. When he conducted seminars on goal setting, he asked attendees to list everything they would like to do over the next 10 years. Surprisingly, this can be done within about 20 minutes or so. Then, he asked everyone to assign the numbers 1, 3, 5, or 10 to each item listed, depending on how many years they feel it will take to reach that goal. He invited them to choose the top four goals for each time period. Finally, he asked them to write out the reasons they want to accomplish each goal. This was a very valuable exercise.

For setting goals the acronym SMART is helpful. It stands for specific, measurable, attainable, relevant and time-bound. Examples of such goals are something like making $100,000 by December 31, 2015, or going to Walt Disney World by Christmas. Goals need these attributes to be effective.

According to Mark Fisher, author of *Instant Millionaire*, "Life gives us exactly what we ask from it." This is more than just a philosophy. To understand this, ask yourself exactly what *you* want in life. As Fisher notes, "If your request is vague, whatever you get will be just as muddled. If you ask for the minimum, you'll get the minimum." He goes on to say, "If you don't ask for anything, you won't get anything." This is why it is critical for you to put your mission statement, values, and goals in writing. By putting them in writing, you are forced to be exact and specific. Fisher says, "The world is but a reflection of your inner self." A reflection can only be as clear as the initial image.

You must act on your own plan. Otherwise, you run the risk of becoming a part of someone else's plan. Sometimes, it can be a very terrible plan and can ruin your life. In this journey of life, we are either wanderers or travelers. Make sure you are traveling on the road *you* want, to a destination *you* have chosen, on *your* map. In other words, make sure you find your focus.

Author Ben Stein is fond of saying, "The indispensable first step to getting the things you want out of life is this: decide what you want." If you aren't sure what you want, eliminate the options you *don't* want and then choose from what remains. Devote yourself to that option and stay with it. If it becomes clear to you that you want something else, then you can change your path. In the process, you learn the basics that can make you a better person and clarify your life's purpose. You never know—by acting instead of waiting, you might just tip the scales and achieve success.

Tools for a Successful Life

Whether you think that you can, or that you can't, you are usually right.

–Henry Ford

Some time ago, I was traveling on Canada 3000, Canada's discount airlines, headed for Los Angeles. As we were over the Pacific Ocean, the pilot made an announcement: "Ladies and gentlemen, we are having a bit of trouble with engine number one. This will delay our arrival into LAX by about 20 minutes. There is nothing to worry about since we have another engine." Later, the pilot came on the air again and said, "Since we are having problems with engine number two, I decided to issue crash landing instructions, just in case. All passengers who know how to swim move to the left side of the cabin. All those who do not know how to swim move to the right side of the cabin. In the event of a crash landing into the water, I would ask the passengers on the left side of the cabin to jump out and swim like hell. For those passengers on the right side of the cabin, let me say thank you for traveling Canada 3000."

Now that is a story about passengers left on their own without any tools for survival! In this chapter, I would like to offer you some key tools to your success so that you are not left to survive on your own. I hope these tools will be of some value to you.

Enthusiasm: Igniting the Flame

The first tool is enthusiasm. Nobody can better describe the importance of this ingredient than Frank Bettger, a best-selling author and former baseball player. According to his obituary, published in the *Philadelphia Inquirer*, Frank started his experience as a baseball player in Johnston, Pennsylvania, in 1906. One day after a game, he was fired by his manager. He was told he was lazy. After drifting through a half-dozen teams, Frank ended up in New Haven, Connecticut, where he was given a trial run in one of the minor leagues. In his book *How I Raised Myself from Failure to Success in Selling*, he relates how his first day in New Haven will always stand out in his memory. He says he acted like a man "electrified"—like he was alive with a "million batteries." He threw the ball so hard to his infielder that it almost tore the man's hands apart. It worked like a miracle. The enthusiasm affected his teammates and he felt better. Ultimately, according to his obituary, his teammates gave him the nickname "Pep" Bettger.

Two years later, Bettger ended up playing first base for the St. Louis Cardinals. Naturally, his income multiplied many times. He attributed his success to "enthusiasm"—that is to say, as the obituary put it, "turning it loose."

Three years later, Frank had a bad accident, which forced him to give up baseball. He became a salesman, selling life insurance. Unfortunately, he was a dismal failure. Then, according to his book, he took a Dale Carnegie class in public speaking. During the class, Frank gave a speech. Right in the middle of it, Carnegie interrupted him. "Are you interested in what you are saying?" he asked.

"Of course I am," replied Bettger.

"Well, why don't you talk with a little enthusiasm?" replied Carnegie. Memories flashed into Bettger's mind about how a lack of enthusiasm threatened to wreck his career in baseball. Bettger decided to put the same enthusiasm into selling that he had put into playing baseball.

On his first call, Bettger became the most enthusiastic salesman possible. He pounded his fist on the table with excitement. Expecting every minute that the prospect would stop him and throw him out of the office, he noticed instead that the prospect raised himself to a more erect position and opened his eyes wider. He didn't throw Frank out! No. In fact, the prospect bought! From that day on, Frank began his climb to become the top salesman for Fidelity Mutual Life Insurance Co.

Frank concludes, "I firmly believe enthusiasm is by far the biggest factor in successful selling." He continues:

> There is just one rule: to be enthusiastic, you have to act enthusiastic. Stand up on your hind legs each morning and repeat, with powerful gestures and with all the enthusiasm you can generate, these words: Force yourself to act enthusiastic and you'll become enthusiastic.

There it is—the power of enthusiasm. But while enthusiasm is important, it is not everything. There are a few other tools you can use to improve yourself.

Affirmations: Picturing Outcomes

Another tool for success is to set a goal and affirm it daily. By using affirmations such as, "I am happy, I am healthy, I am wealthy, I feel good," you begin the process of placing counterweights on the scales of change in your life.

Such affirmations should be in the present tense, should be positive, and should help you see yourself as you want to be. In my case, I have recorded a whole series of affirmations onto a tape with a baroque music background, which plays every morning to wake me up. I use baroque music because studies show that its tempo is the best for reaching into a person's subconscious mind during relaxation. Jack Canfield and Dennis Waitley are two authors who discuss this subject in more depth.

Sentence Stems: Exploring the Mind

A sentence stem is the beginning of a sentence that prompts the user to complete it. Psychologist Nathaniel Branden suggests using the sentence stem, "If I were five percent more _____ this week, I would _____." In the model suggested by Branden, the user inserts the positive quality he or she desires in the first part and then completes the sentence by inserting a word that depicts the behavior that would best achieve the desired result. His idea is that a person can pretty well change anything by at least five percent, and that a week is just the right time frame. For example, if I felt the need for more patience in my life right now, I might say, "If I were five percent more patient this week, I would listen to my wife rather than always interrupting."

Branden suggests you do a minimum of 10 sentence stems a day on each quality you are trying to improve. So, using the "patient" example, you would write at the top of a page the words, "If I were five percent more patient this week." Then you would write the numbers 1 through 10 down the side of the paper. Next, you would write down 10 "action items" (again, for example, "I would listen to my wife rather than always interrupting"), which would get your creative juices flowing.

The theory behind Branden's approach is that you can dredge up a lot of blockage in your subconscious mind and clear it out by using this method. By flushing out psychological roadblocks, you clear the way for your journey to success. The process has the further advantage of clarifying what you must do to achieve your desired result by employing the powers of your conscious and subconscious mind.

Key Questions: Probing the Subconscious

While I am not a member of Alcoholics Anonymous, I admire its "twelve step" program to help recovering alcoholics. One of the steps requires participants to take an inventory at the end of every day to reflect on how well they carried out their day and what impact they made on their own life and the lives of others. This is an exercise from which anyone could benefit.

In my case, for example, I ask myself at the end of each day what was my best achievement. I also reflect on who came into my life that day and what I was grateful for. Finally, I reflect on how I could have done better. The advantage of such questions over affirmations, or probably even sentence stems, is that they probe into your subconscious mind and force it to focus on the most constructive areas of your life.

Mirroring: Copying the Psychological States of Others

According to several practitioners of neuro linguistic programming (NLP), when researchers at Boston University Medical School studied films of people having conversations, they noticed that the people conversing began to unconsciously coordinate their movements, including finger movements, eye blinks and head nods. Moreover, when the people were monitored using electroencephalographs, it was found that some of the subjects' brain waves were spiking at the same moment.

While I was unable to confirm the existence of this study, it is nonetheless widely known in NLP circles and elsewhere that people mirror each other in conversations. Knowing this can be helpful in dealing with others.

To *mirror* is to mimic the physiological state of the person with whom you are interacting. You copy their voice pattern, their breathing rhythm, their mannerisms, etc. Anthony Robbins describes just how effective mirroring can be in the following example from his book, *Awakening the Giant Within You*:

> I was in New York recently, and…went to Central Park. I walked over and sat on a bench….Pretty soon, I noticed this guy sitting across from me. And I just began to mirror him. I'm sitting the way he is, breathing the way he is, doing the same thing with my feet….Then he glances up, and I glance up….Before too long he gets up and walks over to me….We start talking, and I'm mirroring his tone of voice and his phraseology exactly. After a few moments,

he says, "It's obvious you're a very intelligent man." Why does he believe that? Because he feels I'm just like him. Before too long, he's telling me he feels he knows me better than people he's known for twenty-five years. And, not long after that, he offers me a job.

Discipline: Consistent Self-Improvement

Each of these approaches merits consideration. Each offers a tool to use on the road to achievement. None of them, however, is a substitute for discipline—self-discipline, that is. Self-discipline, or the effort to improve one's self as a human being, is the hallmark of all successful people. Success requires discipline to move from the affirmation of a goal to the triumph of its accomplishment. Discipline translates dreams into achievements.

THE POWER OF BURNING DESIRE

Great works are not performed by strength but by perseverance.

–Samuel Johnson

In his book *Think and Grow Rich*, author Napoleon Hill talks about his son, who was born without any physical sign of ears. The doctor admitted to Hill that the child might be deaf and mute for life.

At that moment, Hill made a decision. He knew his son would hear and speak. Although he did not communicate that decision openly, it was nonetheless the decision he made at that time. More than anything else, he desired that his son should not be a deaf mute. Right then and there, he resolved to find a way to transplant into that child's mind and existence his own burning desire for some way to change the situation.

The boy went through grade school, high school, and college without being able to hear his teachers except when they shouted loudly at close range. His parents did not allow the boy to learn sign language because they believed that he should try to live his life as normally as possible and associate with "normal" children. They stood by that decision, despite the enormous cost they paid in arguments with school officials.

In high school, the boy tried an electrical hearing aid, but it had no value. However, he reached a turning point in his life during his last week in college. It happened when he came into possession of another electrical hearing device. Because of his disappointment with the earlier device, he did not rush to try it. But when he did finally place it on his head and hook up the battery, suddenly, as if by a stroke of magic, he could hear!

For the first time in his life, he could hear everything, almost as if he had normal hearing. He called his mother on the telephone, and could hear her clearly. The next day, in class, he was able to hear the voice of his professors for the very first time. His world completely changed.

Napoleon Hill summarizes this experience as follows:

> When I planted in his mind the desire to hear and talk and live as a normal person, there went with that impulse, some strange influence which caused nature to become the bridge builder, and span the gulf of silence between his brain and the outer world. Verily, there is nothing right or wrong which belief and burning desire cannot make real. These qualities are free to everyone.

So they are, and that means we can put them to good use in our careers!

In the beginning, starting any job, professional practice, or even a business is an act of faith. Yes, you must prepare a plan, but when the moment comes, you must simply wade out into the world and take a stand. A plan is helpful, but life seldom follows our plans.

To draw an analogy from the world of football, if you are in the final minute of the Super Bowl and the score is tied, your coach may call the quarterback over to the player's bench to come up with a strategy. That is probably a good idea. But no matter what strategy the team adopts, once the ball is hiked, chaos reigns, and the strategy pretty much goes out the window. That's just life. It does not mean you should not plan, but it does mean that in addition to a plan, it helps if you believe in yourself and have a burning desire to win.

You may very well encounter chaos in the first few days at a new job or when you open the doors to your business or private practice for the first time. Be ready for it. Approach it with the conviction that you will succeed no matter what. It is your dedication and belief in yourself that will carry the day.

The Challenge of Change

For a list of all the ways technology has failed to improve the quality of life, please press three.

–Alice Kahn

Sometimes, it is helpful to look back at where you came from to get a better idea of where your life is headed. With that in mind, I thought it might be useful to share a few reflections on how my profession, and probably many others, changed over the years.

In 1972, before graduating from law school, I often studied in the Henry Angus building at the University of British Columbia in Vancouver, Canada. There was a whole group of us—a few law students, a half dozen business students, and one guy, Sandy McTavish, who was taking computer science.

Sandy was a "geek," and we used to snicker at him behind his back. Nobody quite appreciated what Sandy was doing. Every morning, he would collect a batch of computer cards and review them at his desk, cursing when he found something that didn't work out right. Every evening, after drawing out a whole ream of computer charts and diagrams, he took his cards to the mainframe on campus, where he fed them into the computer.

None of us saw any future for him. Today, however, he is probably high up somewhere in corporate America, laughing at all of us.

Later that year, when I started practicing law in Toronto, secretaries were still typing on IBM Selectric typewriters and used carbon paper to make copies of their work. We used law libraries to find new cases. Having heard this, you probably think I started working in the dark ages, but to me, it feels like my first years in law were only a few months ago. I have no doubt that your career will go by just as quickly, and that 30 years or so from now you will look back with wonder at how things changed since you started.

During the course of my career, my profession faced the assault of new technology and adapted as quickly as it could. After IBM Selectric typewriters, I remember learning how to operate the copier and getting my first Wang word processor with a daisy wheel printer. Then came fax machines and another learning curve. Then computers, then the Internet, emails, scanners, websites, palm pilots, BlackBerries, and smartphones—all these again demanding mastery.

Throughout all these changes in technology, I kept up by going to computer classes, reading books, and studying the new equipment after hours. If you ever spent a few hours trying to fix your computer after a crash in the midst of an important project, you will have some sense of the feelings these new products generated in many of us as they came to market!

As challenging as learning technology was, that was only half the battle. In the same period of time, the practice of law was turned completely inside out. Apart from the virtual explosion of case law and of legislative changes in every legal field with which we had to keep pace, the very essence of practicing law was evolving.

Entire law libraries were converted to digital information on the Internet. Legal software programs dealing with client management, document handling, time keeping, accounting, and countless other applications—not to mention legal resources like West Law and LexisNexis—changed everything. The use of voicemail and emails revolutionized communications in the profession.

Today, the answer to virtually any legal question can be found on the Internet. Legal forms are filled out on a computer in multiple copies, with automatic formatting and carry-over information from form to form. E-filing and court searches for documents over the Internet allow access to the law for anyone, anywhere.

And there is much more to come. Whether we are considering law or any other profession, each person must learn to deal with such improvements. To me, this learning curve has been truly staggering, but nothing compared to what the future is likely to bring.

If you had taken me aside 30 years ago and told me I would be working with a method of communication that had not yet even been invented (i.e., email), using a method of research that was not yet in existence (i.e., the Internet), and carrying around my Rolodex and schedule in a palm-sized electronic apparatus that would also double as a telephone (i.e., my smartphone), I would have seriously questioned your sanity. But it has all come to pass.

Today, I use most of this technology in my work. About 60 percent of my practice involves emailing—responding to clients or passing on directions to my staff on what should be done next—and Internet-based researching. (This is amazing because, as I mentioned, when I went to law school the Internet did not even exist!) The rest is answering phone calls and preparing or reviewing visa applications.

A key to my style of practice has been my website, www.myworkvisa.com. There, I connected all the relevant Web links I need to find forms, information, government departments, and law in the U.S. and Canada. I hired people to build this for me because I didn't know how to do that.

A second key for me is carrying a flash drive with me at all times, where I store precedents to use in my everyday work. This is where I keep a legal services agreement that clients must sign before I commence work for them. These days, cloud computing is also becoming more popular. In addition, far more collaboration with people at different ends of the earth is taking place daily. While these trends are to be welcomed, as we become more interdependent we also become more vulnerable and need to pay attention to cyber security.

I have no doubt that as radical as these changes were in my career, the same is true for people in all the other professions. Recently, my doctor told me that his practice now is like "a scene out of *Star Wars*" due to the technological advancements that have taken place in his profession. Likewise, I have friends who work with engineers and architects who do AutoCAD computer programming. When they entered the business a few decades ago, there was no such thing. Teachers in schools now use computers, which is a far cry from the *Little House on the Prairie* days! The areas affected by change are endless, and the changes are ever more rapidly occurring.

I fully realize that as soon as this book is published, the technological tools that I use will be out of date. In a few years, they will likely be laughable. But that only goes to underline my main point about how quickly things are changing. That is why it only makes sense to adopt an open mind and a willingness to continue learning in your professional life. And by the way, if you think I am ancient, just wait—if you're lucky, soon you will be, too. You won't believe how quickly your career will go by.

Finding Your First Job

Work is an extension of personality. It is achievement. It is one of the ways in which a person defines himself, measures his worth, and his humanity.

–Peter Drucker (1977)

While there are entire books written on this subject, there are a few comments I would like to make with respect to young professionals looking for their first position. Unless you have some contacts, three critical items will determine whether or not you find work. The first is your cover letter, the second is your résumé, and the third is your interview.

Your Cover Letter

As for the cover letter, its entire purpose is simply to introduce the résumé, draw attention to your unique value to this employer, and ask for an interview. That's it. Nothing more. The résumé is obviously the more important of the two items.

Your Résumé

As a young man, I prepared what I thought was a reasonably good résumé. One day, however, I came across the résumé of a friend of mine, Professor Bohdan Krawchenko from the University of Alberta.

He was someone I had worked with for many years. As I reviewed his résumé, I was struck by the concrete detail with which he outlined events in which I had been involved. He presented the same events in a much more professional manner than I had ever done with my résumé.

That made a profound impression on me. At that time, I didn't think of a résumé as anything very significant. But I made up my mind at that moment that I was going to improve my résumé and to make it as good as, or similar to, Professor Krawchenko's.

Your résumé is a statement about how you see your role in life. A few years after my Krawchenko Revelation, I decided to summarize in a short form my major strengths as a person. I thought I would take a novel approach and write this on the back of my business card. I figured if I put my résumé on the back of a business card, it would be concise and unique, and people would appreciate it. Here is what I wrote:

> Member of the Bar of the State of New York, in the United States, Provinces of Ontario, British Columbia, and Alberta in Canada.

> 15 years' legal experience. Exposure to all areas of business in North America. Assisted entrepreneurs, immigrants, and refugees from all over the world.

> Involvement in personal injury and civil litigation. Former Canadian Human Rights Commission Tribunal Panel Member. Former United Nations Correspondent.

That was the best encapsulation I could prepare of my purpose or role in life. It took quite a bit of effort to reduce my résumé to those few sentences.

Then something propelled me to take a deeper look into myself. I had an opportunity to apply for a job as a Consul General for Canada. In doing that, I had to prepare a new résumé and revise my definition of myself. I went to great pains to redefine myself in ways that would be most beneficial for the role that I was hoping I might get. I even spent $150 to get a laser-printed copy of my résumé, which I submitted with my application. This experience helped bring home the fact that your self-definition must always be undertaken with a view of where you want to go in the world.

It is important to seek advice from senior members of your profession in preparing a résumé. Among the most important things they will tell you is that a résumé should not be longer than one page. In most instances, this is a challenge. But this is almost like a rite of passage. Reducing your experience onto one page helps you focus and makes it easier for your prospective employer to identify your uniqueness. Remember: A résumé is merely a way of opening the door for an interview. It is nothing more. You do not have to express your whole life history in a résumé; that is not what a résumé is designed to do.

I learned this the hard way. I thought that as a lawyer who had graduated from law school and taken the bar, I knew how to write a résumé. Wrong. I handed out my résumé again and again only to be rejected. One of the best things you can do after graduation is to put in the effort to preparing a solid résumé.

Of course, you could always get lucky and land a job without doing this. But why search in a garbage can for a few bread crumbs? Why not go to the bakery? Why not get a few books on how to write a good résumé and do it? Your chances of landing the job you want will be greatly improved!

To help you along, I have included a copy of my own résumé at the end of this chapter. I'm not saying it's perfect, but it gives you some idea of what I've learned on this subject. Note the quantification of activities and the specifics included in it.

The Interview

In addition to writing a cover letter and résumé, you'll also need to prepare for job interviews. Although the topic of preparing for an interview merits a book in itself, here I simply suggest that you have the answers to the following five questions:

- ❖ Tell me about yourself.
- ❖ Why should we hire you for this job?
- ❖ Why are you the ideal applicant for this job?
- ❖ What are your weaknesses?
- ❖ Why did you leave your previous position?

I assume you know basics like dressing properly and maintaining eye contact during the course of the interview. But what else should you consider? The following examples, taken from a survey of personnel executives at 200 Fortune 1000 companies, provide some guidance as to what *not* to do during an interview:

- ÷ "When I gave him my business card at the beginning of the interview, he immediately crumpled it and tossed it in the wastebasket."

- ÷ "[The applicant] had arranged for a pizza to be delivered to my office during a lunch-hour interview. I asked him not to eat it until later."

- ÷ "He sat down opposite me, made himself comfortable, and proceeded to put his foot up on my desk."

- ÷ "She actually showed up for the interview during the summer wearing a bathing suit. She said she didn't think I'd mind."

- ÷ "Without asking if I minded, he casually lit a cigar and then tossed the match onto my carpet—and couldn't understand why I was so upset."

If you are anything like me, you would be appalled to encounter someone in any of these scenarios. Hopefully, you know enough to avoid making such obvious mistakes!

Over the years, I have learned that my key consideration in hiring is the person's character. Usually, I form a first impression of the person's character in a matter of a few minutes. Often that impression remains true and determines the fate of the person being hired.

ANDY J. SEMOTIUK
555 Main St., Suite 100, Los Angeles, CA 90042
(123) 555-6900 – Office

Senior-level attorney with strong communication and people skills experienced in immigration law, general management, leadership, organization, and international business projects

Skills Profile

Law
- Member of the bars of California and New York in the U. S.; Ontario, Alberta, and B.C. in Canada
- Former Chairman, Networking Committee, Beverly Hills Bar Association

Communication and People Skills
- Professional speaker
- Former United Nations correspondent
- Former Canadian public television producer. Helped over 10,000 clients in the areas of business, law, and finance

General Management, Leadership, and Organization
- Chairman of the Board and Founding Partner of a law firm with $ 1.2 million annual revenues
- Led campaign that raised $ 2.5 million for a community college
- Held senior positions in various national philanthropic organizations
- Campaign manager in four political campaigns involving thousands of volunteers

International Business Projects
- Lead negotiator on a joint venture light airplane factory built in Beijing, China

Professional Experience

Head, Immigration Section
Manning, Marder & Wolfe, Los Angeles (1999 to present): Established an immigration practice in this 50-attorney law firm with offices in Los Angeles, San Francisco, San Diego, and Irvine, and led its effort to diversify from civil defense to a general practice.

General Counsel
Hansma and Associates, Edmonton, Canada (1997–1998): Assumed leadership of this busy commercial and real estate law practice to relieve owner for a long-term leave. Successfully carried on practice entailing supervision of 300 corporate minute books and completion of several hundred commercial and real estate transactions.

Associate Attorney
First Street Law Office, Edmonton, Canada (1996–1997): Conducted a full-time general law practice with three other senior attorneys in a joint law office while shuttling back and forth between Edmonton and Los Angeles to take courses, study, prepare for, and write the California state bar examinations.

CEO and Owner
Law Office of A. Semotiuk, Edmonton, Canada (1991–1996): Carried on a general law practice while traveling worldwide to speak on business and immigration themes. Led business delegations to Eastern Europe to help with translations. Co-founded and helped to build the $ 2.75 million, 18-hole River Ridge Golf Course in Edmonton.

Partner
Biamonte, Cairo & Shortreed, Edmonton (1985–1990): While practicing with eight partners and five associates, led extensive negotiations for WT Aircraft Manufacturing Ltd. in China.

Previous experience includes the United Nations and practicing law in New York and Toronto.

Starting a Practice

Start by doing what's necessary, then what's possible, and suddenly you are doing the impossible.

–St. Francis of Assisi

In Canada, where I first began the practice of law, the system for training attorneys is different than in the United States. Canada is somewhat of a hybrid when it comes to the marked divisions between barristers and solicitors in the United Kingdom and the American attorney model. In the U.K., if you are a barrister, you are essentially a litigator and nothing else. If you are a solicitor, you do transactional work or briefings for barristers on cases but you do not go to court. Canadian attorneys are both barristers and solicitors at the same time. But the key difference in relation to the American model is the system of articling that both Canada and the United Kingdom employ. The closest American concept would be internship for doctors. In Canada, before I could become a barrister and solicitor, I had to spend a year practicing under the watchful eye of a senior member of the bar. Following that, I wrote my bar exams and ultimately became a lawyer.

Raised in this tradition, I found it amazing that the American legal system would allow attorneys, straight from law school and bar exams, to go out and start their own practices. I can't imagine how a new attorney in the United States can survive like that. But they do. Often it is because there are no better alternatives. Not everyone graduating with a professional degree is courted to join a big firm. The reality is not always as glamorous as television would have you believe. In other cases, it is because these newly minted attorneys know exactly what they want to do and simply cannot wait to get out on their own.

Whether forced to by circumstances or wanting to break free of others, many young people in law and in other professions are courageous enough to give private practice a try. So I thought I would touch on a few themes that might help these individuals, not to mention those who start up as employees of larger organizations.

When I first started my own practice—that is to say, when I bought out a law practice in Edmonton, Alberta—I was not sure what to expect. For one thing, I never looked over the financial statements of the practice. I just assumed that the previous earnings of the owner would continue on once I took over. Thus, I anticipated a cash flow similar to what the former owner had enjoyed. This didn't pan out. In the first month of my practice, my overhead was over just $20,000. I didn't think this was extraordinarily important, although my billings were only about $4,000. I thought things would improve. Wrong!

In the next month, the overhead was around $17,000, but my billings were down to about $3,000. This continued for a couple of months. Needless to say, I went into the red. The result was that I finally had to consolidate my practice, cut back my expenses, and then spend a long period of time recovering. This experience led me to rethink how I would do things if I ever did this again. This chapter summarizes those thoughts.

Obviously, the place to start before purchasing or starting a practice is to project what your revenue is going to be per month, and then project your expenses. If the expenses are likely to exceed the revenue, then they have to be cut back. In essence, what we are talking about here is preparing a business plan. This plan has to describe on paper what the practice is going to be doing, what kind of work will be brought in, how much is expected in the way of revenue from what kind of clients, and how much the expenses are likely to be. The projections should be monthly projections for one year, then quarterly projections for three years. These projections can be revised once you get a better sense of where the practice is going.

Here is an outline of the key elements to a good business plan, adapted from the framework suggested by the U.S. Small Business Administration.

Elements of a Business Plan

1. Executive Summary
2. Statement of Purpose
3. Table of Contents

I. The Practice
   A. Description of Practice
   B. Marketing
   C. Competition
   D. Operating Procedures
   E. Personnel
   F. Practice Insurance
   G. Financial Data

II. Financial Data
   A. Loan Applications
   B. Capital Equipment and Supply List
   C. Balance Sheet
   D. Break-Even Analysis
   E. Pro-Forma Income Projections (Profit and Loss Statements)
      Three-Year Summary
      Detail by Month, First Year
      Detail by Quarters, Second and Third Years
      Assumptions upon Which Projections Were Based
   F. Pro-Forma Cash Flow
      Follow Guidelines for Letter E

III. Supporting Documents
   A. Tax Returns of Principals for Last Three Years
   B. Personal Financial Statement (All Banks Have These Forms)
   C. Copy of Proposed Lease or Purchase Agreement for Building Space
   D. Copy of Licenses and Other Legal Documents
   E. Copy of Résumés of All Principals
   F. Copies of Letters of Intent from Suppliers, Etc.

Brian Tracy, a leading management consultant and speaker in the United States, says that whenever he is invited to consult with a company, the first thing he tries to do is to clarify the company's purpose. "What is it you are trying to do?" he asks. Clear thinking and agreement about the purpose of any organization is essential to good management. The same can be said about any practice and its business plan. The plan helps to clarify your thinking, and gaining agreement on the plan with your personnel helps to prevent you from working at cross-purposes. The key is to get it down on paper.

Make up a Schedule of Fees

When you go to McDonald's, the first thing you see is the menu with prices. Without that menu and price list, you would have to ask the attendant, who might have to guess what the price of a hamburger is. This would lead to utter confusion and ultimate bankruptcy. That menu, together with the pricing, is what makes it possible for McDonald's to do business with its customers. In any professional practice, you must determine what services you will provide and set your prices.

Some professions require that you charge a certain price for your services. For example, the medical profession is highly regulated in terms of what services practitioners can provide and what fees they can charge. There may be areas in your practice where you have to charge a tariff that is set by your profession. For example, the fees charged on an estate in the legal profession must be exactly what everybody else charges. But elsewhere—and this really applies to most professions and most services—you have to set a competitive fee. My area, immigration law, is highly competitive and works like that. I have to be sensitive to what my competition is charging and adjust my fees to the market rates. The best way to do this is to use the Internet to find competitor fee schedules. It used to be difficult to find out what your competition was charging. Sometimes, you had to make agreements to survey your colleagues and ultimately develop a fee schedule or rely on employment agencies that would provide such statistics. With the advent of the Internet, this has all changed. Most pricing can be obtained by doing a search of fees that people have published.

A lot of people are very skilled at getting you to work for them for free. One night, when I was working in Canada, I spoke about fees with my principal, Yaroslaw Botiuk, a seasoned barrister and solicitor in Toronto. He looked at one of the files I was working on, where I had spent a lot of time for a client before the client had paid us, and he said, "We don't work for free here." Although rather direct, that was a lesson I needed to learn. Like at McDonald's, first you pay, and then you get the hamburger. This is a good practice to follow.

Banking

Now let's talk about what you are going to do with all that money you are going to make in your practice. Let's talk basic banking. One of the most important relationships you will establish in your practice is the one you develop with your banker. Choosing a good bank manager to deal with is important. As a professional, you will have unique financial needs. Not every bank manager will truly understand those needs. Following are some things to consider in choosing the right bank.

Does the Bank Understand Your Unique Cash-Flow Situation?

All banks offer checking and savings accounts. However, a professional practice is not like many other businesses. Professionals have unique cash-flow needs because of monthly fluctuations in client payments. A good bank recognizes the difference and will help the professional facilitate cash management and maximize the value of cash deposits. For example, your bank might offer online banking, money market accounts earning higher interest rates on deposits, and overdraft protection. While it is important to read the fine print about the product features, interest rates and monthly fees, it is even more important to have a trustworthy banker who will act in your best interests in these areas.

When You Need a Loan, Will You Be Able to Get One?

What sets a great bank apart from a good one is its understanding of how professionals like you work. This understanding is especially important should you need a sizeable loan for a new acquisition, a seasonal disruption, or an unforeseen expense. For example, traditional banks typically require tangible assets as collateral for a business loan. The problem is most professionals don't have much to show in tangible assets. In the absence of inventory or equipment to secure a loan, professionals may be required to pledge their homes or other personal assets. The solution is to look for a lender that understands your practice's size and strength. They will be more likely to take into account your practice's history, the relative stability of its cash flow, the strength of your client relationships, and its ongoing potential. This can make all the difference when you need capital to expand, buy out a competitor, or strengthen your economic base.

Is the Bank Your Trusted Business Partner or Just a Transaction Manager?

Does your bank really care about you? What level of service does your practice command at the bank? Of course, you expect accuracy and quick processing. But the real measure of a bank's service to your practice is its ability to help you solve financial problems. First off, is your banker accessible? Does he or she understand your business well enough to recommend financial efficiencies? The bottom line is, do you consider your banker a valued and trusted advisor, dedicated to the financial vitality of your operation? If not, you may be better served by a bank more focused on customer service.

You Do Have a Choice!

If you're not happy with your current bank or wonder if there's one better suited to your practice, the important thing to know is that you have a choice. You don't have to stay with your current bank just because it is comfortable or convenient. Making the switch may take some time and effort, but it could be one of the most important decisions you make in helping your practice grow and succeed.

Two Accounts

When you start off with a bank, you need to set up two bank accounts: a trust account and a general bank account. The trust account is where you put client money that is not yet earned and therefore not yet yours. An example of this is where a client pays you money in advance for work to be done. The money is placed into trust until the work is completed. When you bill your work out at your normal hourly rate, you may transfer funds from the trust account to your general account to pay yourself.

A key to good professional banking is to ensure that all funds you receive and all funds you pay out are processed through your trust account, your general account, or both. With respect to deposits into your trust account or your general account, you should always photocopy the check that you have received. On your photocopy, you should put your signature, the date that you received the check, and into which account it has been deposited. Keep the photocopy in the client's file. I even photocopy cash and treat that copy the same way. As for direct or bank wire deposits, adopt a standard practice and follow it. For example, you might ensure that such deposits are always made into a special bank account used only for this purpose. The funds can then be transferred to the account in which they belong without problems related to bank charges, accounting errors, currency conversion costs, or interest accrued.

Any amount that you pay out should be paid only on receipt of an invoice or statement of account equal to the amount of the check. If you have no statement of account or invoice, *you make no payment*. When you pay an invoice off, you should mark the date it was paid on the invoice or statement of account, the check number you used to pay it, the amount of the check, and the signature of the person who signed the check. This applies to all payments, whether from your trust account or your general account.

Again, remember to photocopy all deposits, and make it a practice not to make any payment until you receive a statement of account or invoice. With respect to minor expenses that you may incur, such as miscellaneous expenses for postage or office supplies, you can pay out a miscellaneous amount not to exceed, say, $100 in cash, and then account from time to time for the $100 before paying out a further $100 for miscellaneous expenses.

As long as you follow this paper flow with respect to all payments, your accountant will easily be able to prepare your financial statements, and you will never have any trouble. Keeping on top of your trust and general accounts in this way is critical to staying afloat in business. Using an accounting program like QuickBooks can also help you in this regard.

Not long ago, John Williams, a friend of mine, was in the lobby of a restaurant in West L.A. when Donald Trump walked in. John introduced himself and told Trump he was meeting some very important business clients who he wanted to impress. He asked Trump to come over to his table during the lunch and say hello. Trump agreed. During lunch, Trump made his way over and said, "John Williams, how are you? Aren't you going to introduce me to your friends?" John answered, "Not now, Donald. We're eating. Come back later."

That story illustrates that just because you are trying to get clients doesn't mean you can afford to neglect important people. Don't neglect your banker, your accountant, and other important matters when you start up your practice. Get started on the right foot.

Selling Your Professional Services

*If you can do anything better than anybody else, this old country is
so constituted they want to see you get all you can out of it.*

–Will Rogers (1925)

Early in my career, I was captivated by the success of the Pet Rock. This was a cute idea that encouraged consumers to buy a nicely packaged rock and care for it like a pet. I understood why people bought hula-hoops, but this Pet Rock thing was something altogether different. Nonetheless, it became clear to me that the reason people were buying these Pet Rocks was because of the story and the romancing of the concept in the media. I decided I could come up with a better idea.

My invention was the solar energy clothes dryer. It was a piece of rope in a box with an instruction booklet that was humorous in nature. I came up with what I thought were some great lines poking fun at the idea that the purchaser had bought a piece of rope to hang clothes on called the "Solar Energy Clothes Dryer." I then went to work trying to market the product. I made 100 boxes and started approaching purchasers all over Western Canada and in the United States.

Unlike the guy who invented the Pet Rock, however, I had no knowledge of marketing and I had no distribution system. I also had very few resources to put behind my product. The result was predictable.

The product went nowhere, and the project folded after a few weeks. But I learned something from that experience, a truth that applies to all sales:

> All sales have to begin with a need. The stronger the need, the more likely the sale.

If you don't have a headache, it doesn't matter how cheaply I will sell you an aspirin. You simply won't buy it. But if you have a colossal headache after a three-day binge, one aspirin can be invaluable. The point is to find someone with a need, and then fill it.

Not everyone who walks into your workplace will have a need—or a strong enough need—for your services. So the starting point is to find clients with strong needs. Your job is not to prevail on clients, insisting that they take your services. Instead, you should be an assistant buyer for your client, helping the client meet his or her needs by offering to show the client what services you have that meet those needs.

In any sales situation, including marketing professional services, the client will always ask three questions. The client will want to know about you, about your company, and about your service.

Many years ago Kathleen Harrison Todd, a friend of mine who taught lawyers, told me that she was astounded by the fact that very few lawyers could look her in the eye while they were talking with her. This was critical because eye contact is a means of building trust, and trust is the first ingredient to the successful development of clients. So make sure you maintain eye contact while speaking with clients. It's how the client will learn about you.

The client also wants to know that your company is solid, and may be skeptical because of the bad experiences he or she may have had with various professionals. It's your job to persuade the client that your firm is reputable, will stand behind its work, and will help him or her. Positive third-party endorsements are valuable because they are an indirect, more credible way of saying the same thing you would say yourself about your firm.

Finally, the client will want to know about your service and whether it meets his or her needs. We are not trying to foist our service on clients or hoodwink them into accepting us; rather, we are trying to persuade the client that our service is the answer to his or her need. Make sure you are dealing with a client who has a real headache before you start selling that person aspirins!

The Boston Coffee Lesson: Achieving Success One Step at a Time

What I am about to share next cost me $50,000 to learn. But I'd like to share it with you for free. I hope you can use it.

In the late 1980s, I was approached by a few individuals to join them in a venture involving the coffee business. Four of us agreed that we would embark on a business venture aimed at replacing Starbucks as the principal coffee supplier in North America. Our company was called Boston Coffee, and we started with one coffee cart serving espresso coffee at the Hilton Hotel in downtown Edmonton. Each of us invested our time, knowledge, and money to make the dream a success.

Initially, things seemed to go well. People warmed up to our coffee cart, and we started getting regular customers. Even visiting NHL hockey players grew accustomed to visiting our cart before their games. We started looking at different coffee places, purchasing coffee at lower prices, and researching everything necessary to build our joint enterprise. We focused on buying coffee equipment, buying coffee beans, marketing Boston Coffee, dealing with personnel, accounting, legal issues, signing leases, and more. The one thing we *failed* to focus on, however, was providing the finest cup of coffee to the customer, every day.

Day after day, coffee cup by coffee cup, our business sank into the ground because of our neglect. People soon realized that our coffee was no good and they stopped buying. And they were right to stop buying; we were serving substandard coffee. As a result, our venture folded.

But there was something to be learned from this experience: Focus on the one thing you provide daily and do the best possible job you can with what you have in front of you. Everything else will grow as a result of your good service.

Your Price Is Too High

Some professions are so regulated that the subject of price never comes up. But most professions are not so regulated. In these professions, this objection to engaging our services—that is, the price being too high—is so frequent that it is worth talking about.

Whenever you are told your price is too high, ask the potential client why he or she wants to change the status quo. Elicit information on what is unbearable about it. Ask how much this hurts the client financially, physically, or emotionally. Imagine piling up these answers on one side of a scale to tip it from the negative objection weighing the other side down.

The objection about price really boils down to the potential client saying, "You haven't convinced me of the benefits of your services." When you hear price, it's time for the "why?" questions. Why did you contact me? Why do you want to change your current situation? Why do you want to move forward? The answers to these questions illustrate to the client the benefits of dealing with you. That's why the price of your services should always be the last thing discussed.

Again, we are not here to try to hoodwink someone into using our service. We are looking for clients with real needs. These questions are simply devices to help a potential client with a real need make up his or her mind.

In the end, once you've been engaged, the best technique is to do a sensational job. Always try to give the client more than he or she bargained for. Putting it another way, always promise less than you will deliver. Be faithful to your client, and treat the client as one of your best friends. Even in those instances where a person decides not to be your client, always try to give him or her something—some advice or helpful suggestion to solve a problem or at least point the person in the right direction to find the solution.

Professional Practice: The Nuts and Bolts

*I am of certain convinced that the greatest heroes are those
who do their duty in the daily grind of domestic affairs
whilst the world whirls as a maddening dreidel.*

–Florence Nightingale

Writing Office Memos and Letters

One of the first things I learned in an office was to write a memo. Today, emails have virtually replaced this method of communication, but they share the same format as that used in memo writing. Essentially, what I did not know is that a memo begins from someone and is addressed to someone and it has a subject line, which tells the reader what the memo is going to be about. The memo also has a date. This format was new to me, but it is something that I've used ever since.

It doesn't take long after you enter the professional world to recognize that what is important is not what is said, but what is written. In the world of business, executives confirm everything in writing. Even after reaching an oral agreement with a trustworthy friend, smart executives confirm the terms of the agreement with a follow-up email or sometimes by letter. Putting things in writing helps to get rid of the cobwebs in thinking and clarify the loose ends to focus on what is important. A professional would be wise to follow this same practice.

When it comes to business communication these days, pretty much everything is handled by email. Still, memos are sometimes used for internal organizational matters. When communicating with the outside world on important matters, letters on letterhead are often used. Sometimes, the letter is both sent as an attachment to an email because of the urgency involved as well as sent in the mail in hardcopy form as a follow-up. You will have to pick up the best practices for your own organization or adopt a policy on these matters.

The key to effective writing is to be concise, straightforward, and simple. Great writing is not writing so much as it is rewriting. Rewrite often and try to edit out all repetitive ideas. A good approach is to try to edit one word out of every sentence, one sentence out of every paragraph, one paragraph out of every chapter. Use the active voice and simple language. Try to be informal.

As a general rule, I try to address my letters to the other person using his or her first name. This runs against current convention (although times are changing), but I believe it is a good practice because usually it brings me closer to the recipient. In all my communications I try to tell the recipient why I am writing in the first paragraph. In other words, I tell the recipient what result I want to accomplish by writing to him or her. If I am responding to some earlier correspondence, I usually attach a copy of it for the recipient's convenience and I address whatever points I have to make in the same order as they are addressed in the attached communication. If I am responding by email, I copy the original text into my email reply and intersperse my comments in the body of the original text wherever I need to comment or respond. In such emails, I use bold format and a different font than the one used by the other party. Where there is no prior communication to follow, I try to cover who, what, where, how, why, and when, and present my thoughts in declining order of importance.

Quite often, I first send a draft of the letter I am proposing to write to my client for consideration and review. The client will usually make some good suggestions that will ensure the client's views and thoughts are clearly represented. I then correct the letter and send it out to opposing counsel or wherever it is to go. I find this to be a very helpful practice that prevents later misunderstandings.

My Telephone Log

The following is an example of a breakthrough that Ted Greer, one of my mastermind partners, suggested to me.

I work with a phone log, which is a simple ringed notebook in which I record every phone call that I make. In it, I include the name of the person I'm calling, the phone number, and a brief note about our discussion. I also log incoming calls from clients with a few words concerning the content of the phone call. This helps me enormously, particularly because I travel back and forth between two countries and often need to phone a client and check in with respect to what we discussed the last time we spoke. There are computer programs that you can use to log telephone conversations, such as ACT or other contact-management programs, which are also very effective. Unfortunately, I haven't figured out how to adapt these to my traveling schedule yet. What matters is that you log your discussions in whatever way is best for you.

I find that by using my notebook, I can also log matters that arise during meetings. I do this at the back of the notebook by recording the date of the meeting, where it was held, and its purpose. All of these notes are very useful to me down the road if I ever need to refer to them to remind myself of what occurred. I also use the back of my notebook to plan matters related to my practice.

Dealing with Paperwork

Anybody who starts a practice—or any business, for that matter—will soon be deluged with a massive amount of paperwork. It's important to adopt a procedure to deal with paper flow; doing so can eliminate hours of tedious work.

The procedure I adopted was simply to handle all paperwork only once. As I look at a piece of paper, I choose one of three options:

❖ Delegate.

❖ Destroy it.

❖ File it.

As I look at each piece of paper, I also put my initials and the date on it. This helps me later to remember whether I have seen the page.

When I started practicing on my own, I found that my accountant was providing me with reams and reams of papers reporting on various financial aspects of my practice. There were accounts payable, accounts receivable, bank statements, and everything else under the sun. One day my friend Henry Rutkowski came to see me at the office. Henry, who was in his 60s, had lived through hell in Eastern Europe during World War II. Afterward, he came to Canada to become a multi-millionaire. He knew finance. For example, just before the recession in the 1980s, Henry pulled out all his money from various investments, saving him a fortune, while the rest of us went over the Niagara Falls. But that's another story.

On this particular occasion, Henry sat in my office and pointed to a pile of accounting papers on my desk. "What's that?" he asked. I told him that was my accounting for last month. He smiled and said, "I learned long ago that the key to running a business is to keep your eyes on your general account." He added, "When you are out of money in that account, you are out of business!" It was so simple, but true.

Effective Delegation

When you start off in your career, you will usually do everything yourself. There is no room for delegation because you can't afford to hire people to help you do your work. Even as your practice grows, however, there will be items on your work schedule that you will not be able to delegate. Some things will always require your attention. But eventually, you will be able to delegate at least some things.

To know what should be delegated, ask yourself whether the work involved falls within your unique ability or whether it is work that someone with less ability could do. For example, if you are a brain surgeon, you should not be doing office maintenance.

Once you have identified what should be passed on, there are a few good rules that help to make your delegation effective. The key to good delegation is clarity in giving instructions. I believe it's important to clearly define what you want at the end of the work, and in what time frame you expect it to be done. For example, you might say to someone, "I want you to write a letter to Mr. Wilson about our accounting policy. I would like a draft of this letter by Thursday." (Whenever I delegate such a task to someone, unless that person is a seasoned professional, I ask him or her to do a draft and then I review it. This is particularly true for matters in which I have direct responsibility or when I have special knowledge that other people do not have.)

The *other* key to good delegation is to teach the person what needs to be done by providing him or her with a precedent or model as well as written instructions on how to do it (when possible). In this scenario, you are a teacher. You ask the pupil to take on the work and bring it back for review and corrections. Having done this a few times, you then become a coach. You encourage the delegate to do the work, but you spend less time correcting things and simply check over what has been done to make sure that everything is right. Your job is to encourage confidence in the person to whom the task has been delegated. In time, you will reach a point where you ask the delegate only to check with you if there is a problem with the work and you allow the delegate to freely undertake whatever work he or she wishes. In other words, the process of delegation is from tight control to loose control.

Technology, Accounting, Filing Procedures, and Related Details

As hard as it may be to believe, I am not an expert on everything. (Joke!) Some areas are best left to others. Your best bet for advice on topics like these is to consult your information technology (IT) professional (a key figure in your success team), your accountant, and websites dealing with your area of practice. These nuts-and-bolts matters can quite easily be addressed by speaking with your advisors and with attendants at local business-supply stores.

Planning and Crisis Management

As my practice developed, I realized that I needed to plan more in order to be more effective in my work. At first, I would take one day per week to plan. I found that for each hour of planning, I saved about three hours in the execution of work. I eventually found that I actually only needed half a day at the end of the week to review my week and to project what might happen next week. I also needed to take a day at the end of the month and a couple days at the end of the year to review my work and to reflect on how I could improve. I recommend this for your practice.

In planning your work, it is important to set out your priorities and to list all the matters to which you need to attend in the course of a day, week, and month. Then decide what items on the list are *not* to be done. The true art in planning is not only in deciding what items must be done, but also what items are *not* to be done. It's amazing how many items you might have on the list that you could eliminate, delegate, or simply postpone if you do some planning in advance.

From time to time, I've run into emergencies that needed special care and attention. During those moments, I found it important to stop what I was doing so I could think clearly. The more important and far-reaching the item, the more I found I needed to stop what I was doing and take the time I needed to get out of the office to think about what to do and how to approach the problem.

One day, my banker notified me that he was calling in my line of credit, even though I had partnered with this bank for about 15 years. This prompted a crisis because I didn't know how I was going to carry on and pay all my expenses. In that kind of a situation, it's critical to stop what you are doing, get out of the office, and reflect on how to handle the matter. Even then, I didn't know what to do! Finally, I consulted Henry Wilman, a close friend who is a financial planner. In a few hours, over a couple of coffees, he helped me devise a good financial plan to deal with the crisis. The plan entailed getting a loan at another bank as an interim measure until I could stabilize myself. It worked.

In September 1982, in the course of three days, seven people who consumed Tylenol in the Chicago area died. Tylenol, Johnson & Johnson's number-one product, had been spiked with cyanide. That triggered a national scare that prompted an untold number of people to throw medicine away and stores nationwide to pull Tylenol from their shelves. Today, every time you open a bottle or package of medicine, food, or beverage that is tamper-proof, it is because of that Tylenol case back in 1982. Clearly, this was a life-and-death situation not only for people who used Tylenol, but for the continued existence of Johnson & Johnson itself. This was a *big problem*! How Johnson & Johnson handled it is an invaluable lesson for all of us to this very day.

Case studies on how Johnson & Johnson handled that matter indicate that the company reflected on its values, principles, mission statement, and vision statement, and in doing so were able to decide on a course of action. This course of action ultimately led to their pulling all Tylenol capsules from all stores in the U.S., developing a protective measure with respect to the product, and then marketing the product again. They could have handled it many different ways. However, the way they approached the problem helped to maintain public confidence in its product. As a result, Tylenol remains one of the top products used by consumers as well as by doctors and hospitals for their patients. This is a good example of how to approach any crisis in any organization.

Staying Current in Your Profession

When it comes to staying on top of developments in your profession, I find that the best and most effective approach is to subscribe to newsletters from my competition. In this way, I stay current, and I also know what my competitors are thinking. Currently, I receive about six email newsletters per month covering the whole gamut of immigration law. This is one of my best tips for success in any profession.

In addition to reading competitor newsletters, it is important for you to stay current with your area of practice by reading the literature that pertains to it. If an organization focused on your profession publishes a monthly magazine or newsletter, you should subscribe to it and read it regularly. It's been said that if you read one hour per day in the field that you have chosen, within three years you will be an expert, and within five years you will be a leader.

Sometimes you don't know the answers when it comes to handling a client matter. Even with research, it is sometimes difficult to figure out what to do. In those instances, don't hesitate to book a paid consultation with a top leader in your profession on the subject area you are wrestling to understand. Booking an appointment and actually paying for the consultation will provide you with enormous help.

A similar approach is to contact a leading member of your profession and ask him or her to be your mentor. Some professions actually have mentor programs, in which younger professionals are matched up with senior members of the profession to help them with specific problems. I know that whenever I have been approached to be a mentor, I have always found it very flattering and worthwhile. I am certain other senior members of your profession feel the same way.

A similar suggestion would be to organize a "mastermind" group consisting of a number of professionals in your field who would meet regularly, perhaps to discuss mutual concerns and thereby help each other with problems they face. I have attended regular monthly meetings of just such a group for more than 15 years. While there are books on how to run such mastermind meetings effectively, our group uses a very simple approach. Each month, we share new events in our lives and try to help each other deal with any problems we are facing. Some meetings are very meaningful while others are quite superficial. All the meetings, however, serve to demonstrate our concern for each other. Whatever the form meetings have taken, I found that some of the greatest breakthroughs in my career and my life came as a result of suggestions from my mastermind colleagues.

The Show Must Go On

In time, as your practice grows, so will your responsibility. From time to time, there will be problems that cause worries. I have found that one way of dealing with my worries, particularly when they are keeping me up at night, is to list them in a notebook or diary. I list everything that I can think of. By doing so, I find that I empty my mind of these worries. Soon afterward, I am able to sleep, having dealt effectively with my worries in this way.

In dealing with client matters, from time to time things just won't go the way you want them to go. In those circumstances, it's really important to advise the client as soon as possible about the bad news. If there is a development involving any news—good or bad— you must report it to your client as soon as possible. With respect to bad news, particularly very bad news, it is important to deliver it in person. In these instances, when I have the client come to my office, I sometimes feed that person a piece of candy first to boost his or her blood sugar. That usually raises the person's spirits and makes him or her better able to cope with bad news. I then deliver the bad news. I have found this to be an effective way of minimizing the degree of impact that the bad news has on the client.

Let me conclude with a story. In the late 1980s, my wife and I attended an event at the Kingsway Field House in Edmonton. The event was a multicultural evening, recognizing the various cultures that have made contributions to Canadian society. There must have been about 5,000 people present that night. To start the event, the organizers turned off all the lights. I could not believe how dark it was that evening in that field house. In fact, I mentioned to my wife that it was so dark that I could not see my own hand, which was about a foot away from my face.

At that moment, a spotlight came on our friend Sam Joseph, a thin, older, East Indian man. He was the master of ceremonies that evening. As he walked out onto the runway in front of the stage, he welcomed everybody, speaking while he continued walking forward. Suddenly he just disappeared. For a few seconds, the spotlight was empty. The entire crowd didn't know what had happened. Then, suddenly, Sam appeared in the spotlight again, as if out of nowhere. The show went on without a further hitch.

Later, we learned that Sam had fallen off the end of the platform into the crowd. Luckily, he did not hurt himself. He quickly got back up on to the stage and reappeared in the spotlight. It was one of the most extraordinary events I had ever witnessed.

When you open the doors to your new practice, or even if you start a new job in your profession, you will be in the spotlight. Your staff, suppliers, banker, accountant, IT professional, and all of your clients will be watching you as you perform. The better you do, the more prominent you will become. Sooner or later, however, you will face hardships. They may knock you down. The important thing is to get right back up on your feet and get back into the spotlight. Sam Joseph taught us that lesson—one that few of us who were present that night will ever forget!

Five Key Leadership Concepts for the Professional World

Effective leadership is putting first things first.
Effective management is discipline, carrying it out.

—Stephen Covey

Effective leaders are not born; they are people who have learned to apply sound leadership techniques to their lives as well as their jobs. It is important to realize that no one can be a successful leader unless they first develop the discipline to deal with the ups and downs of their own lives. This chapter discusses how to develop more effective leadership skills.

Give the Customers What They Want

The purpose of a business enterprise is to satisfy customer needs. If it does so, it will grow and prosper. If it doesn't, it will die.

The first step for any business, then, is to give the customers what they want. But here is the key: Give it to them the way they want it. If you serve hamburgers with onions but the customer wants a hamburger without onions, give him the hamburger the way he wants it. If you own a grocery store and your customers ask you for Diet Pepsi when you don't have it, make sure the next time they come back, you do. The measure of your commitment to customer service is the extent to which you will go out of your way to give your customers what they want, the way they want it.

Moments of Truth

Jan Carlsson, the president of SAS Airlines, points out that in any business, there are moments of truth—those instances when the enterprise is in contact with its customers. Customers judge businesses by how well they perform in these moments of truth. Moments of truth are what you should concentrate your efforts on, as they alone will shape your customers' perceptions of you. For example, at SAS, the key moments of truth are reservations, ticketing, check-ins, and baggage handling. This is what they concentrated on to improve their business.

Reward People for Doing Things Right

As Professor Michael Le Boeuf rightly points out, the important thing in any organization is not its philosophy or professed management style, but rather the reward system it employs. Determine what kind of behavior is being rewarded, and you will know which direction the company is moving.

The idea is to align the rewards given to employees with the direction management wants to take the company. The same principle can be applied to modify customer behavior. Reward what you want; ignore what you do not want. As Ken Blanchard says, instead of being on the lookout for what is wrong, "Catch people doing things right," and compliment them on it.

In Toastmasters, we are taught to "sandwich" our feedback when evaluating speakers. We open and close with positive feedback, and sandwich points for improvement in the middle. This is a variation of the same theme.

The Three "A's" of Good Service

Are you in the service industry? Do you know what your clients want? According to Dr. Ken Lawless, in dealing with professionals or people providing services, there are three key factors clients care about.

- ⁜ **Availability.** First and most important, according to research, is the availability of the service provider.
- ⁜ **Affability.** Second, there is the affability of the service provider.
- ⁜ **Ability.** Finally, and only third in importance, is the person's ability.

These three "A's"—availability, affability, and ability—are the crucial factors to pay attention to in service.

Problem Solving

Some problems are beyond us and cannot be solved. The potential destruction of Earth by an errant comet hurtling through space may be a matter of grave concern, but it is something you can do nothing about. Is the problem you face one about which you can do something? If not, leave the problem alone. Let those who *can* do something worry about the problem. Move on to those problems *you* can do something about.

As an attorney, I was trained to put forth the facts in chronological order on paper. As simple as this might sound, it's amazing that many people who struggle with problems never think of putting their thoughts on paper. This exercise forces you to be specific and helps you remove the "fuzziness" from the problem. In medicine, they say that a proper diagnosis (i.e., a proper definition of the problem) is halfway to the cure. So obviously the first step is to define the problem on paper.

The second step is to study and research as much as possible about the problem as well as potential solutions to it. Nowadays, this can be done on your computer using the Internet. But you can also visit the local public library and bookstores. You might also consider consulting an expert who deals in this area. Another excellent source of information and knowledge are audio CD and cassette programs.

If research does not produce an answer to your problem, try making lists of possible solutions. State the problem at the top of a page and then list 20 possible solutions for it. Be creative. Then go over your list and rank the solutions according to their effectiveness in resolving the issue.

Generally speaking, my philosophy is that God helps those who help themselves. Undertaking this process can go a long way toward the solution of any problem. But if you still do not have an answer, try resorting to prayer, meditation, or deep reflection. This helps you tap into your unconscious mind, releases your creative side, and connects you with your spiritual dimension. The key is to believe a solution will present itself, and it will.

A Professional Office

Get action, do things; be sane; don't fritter away your time; create, act, take a place wherever you are and be somebody; get action.

–Theodore Roosevelt (1948)

Professionalism

Napoleon Bonaparte, the famous French leader, attributed his success to arriving 15 minutes early at every meeting. This is a wise adage. If you are unable to abide by this advice, at the very least come on time. This signals that you are a professional.

Professionalism means being on time or, when that is impossible, negotiating with others to enable you to delay a particular matter by agreement. Professionalism means doing a good job, the kind you would want others to do for you. It means keeping the affairs of your clients confidential and not sharing them outside the office. It also means minding your own business and not getting involved in someone else's affairs—unless there is a clear, understandable reason for doing so. Professionalism means respecting other people's time and not wasting it. It also means respecting another person's privacy, even in circumstances when you overhear what they're talking about. Professionalism means if you must criticize someone else, always sandwich your criticism between positive comments about the person's life, behavior, or qualities.

Professionalism also involves abiding by some professional boundaries. Stealing office supplies, using the photocopier for personal use, and gossiping about the private lives of fellow employees are all absolutely wrong. In all these instances, I believe the best policy is to back off. Office romances are a delicate area. There is a saying that applies: "Don't mix business and pleasure." Such relationships tend to poison the office environment, taking the focus off work and instead putting it on what is happening with the new couple and its impact on everyone else. My general advice is, if you get involved in an office romance—especially in situations where you work in a small office, department, or unit—one of you needs to head for the door. There may be exceptions to this rule, but not many.

To summarize, professionalism means being on time, doing a good job, keeping confidential information to yourself, not gossiping, respecting other people's time and property, and avoiding office romances.

Be Sure of Your Own Character and of Those Around You

I encourage you to be the same person you are in front of people as you are behind their backs. This is often difficult to do.

One incident taught me a big lesson in this regard. I was one of the founding partners of a law firm in Edmonton back in the early 1980s. The firm was a merger of three separate law firms. In our merger discussions, we came up with a name reflecting the merger. But in time, many of the partners became unhappy with the firm's name. They felt that one of the partners was not enough of a team player and that his antecedents were a drawback to the new law firm's name. These were the reasons expressed to me as to why we should change the name, and I agreed to carry those arguments forward to a partnership meeting.

At the meeting, an incredible thing happened. The people who had inspired me to lead the attack backed off when the vote was counted. The result was that the name did not change. Needless to say, my actions did not win any popularity contests. I do not fault the other partners because it is very difficult to be open and truthful about reservations that you have about someone else when they are present. Eventually, the partners voted to change the name of the law firm and excluded the relevant partner from the firm. I was the last partner to sign off on those papers.

Later, I developed a friendship with the partner in question, who left. We reconciled with respect to the leadership role I played in attacking him in that partnership meeting. In part, I believe it was because that partner understood that I was the same whether I was talking to him directly or talking about him when he was not present.

I believe that Brian Tracy, a well-know professional speaker and leader in corporate America, has the best approach to dealing with this kind of problem. Brian suggests that in deciding what your behavior should be, you should think of it as being covered on the front page of your city newspaper on the following morning. If you can live with what is said, then go ahead and do it.

Do Not Rush into Action

Napoleon Bonaparte followed the practice of gathering all the letters that came to him in a pile and then opening them once every three months or so. This strange practice actually has some merit to it. A lot of the communication we receive appears to be urgent, but in actual fact can be resolved by itself.

I am amazed when I go away on vacation that urgent problems that occur while I am away somehow resolve themselves so that when I return, they are no longer problems. Not always, but it happens.

Be Aware of the Problems of Alcohol

One of the most difficult problems a young professional practice can face is when one of the principals struggles with alcoholism. This was a problem we addressed at our law firm in the 1980s. One of our partners suffered from the illness of alcoholism. It became increasingly apparent that he was drinking on the job, and we as partners grew increasingly concerned about whether he could manage his own affairs and what impact his illness would have on the affairs of our clients.

Alcohol is such a pervasive element in our social and business environments that it can create an insurmountable obstacle for the alcoholic who has to participate in meetings and social gatherings where drinking is part of that function. In our case, at retreats and follow-ing partner meetings, the partners would pull out the alcohol as part of their social interactions. I believe this was devastating for the alco-holic. I believe it took great courage for him to somehow try to cope in this environment.

In partnership meetings, we discussed his illness and the fact that we were not a social welfare organization. We were there to make a profit. At least, that is the way I argued it. Of all the partners, I believe I was the hardest on him. I remember meetings with him in which I confronted him about his drinking and argued that he needed to stop for the sake of both himself and his family. I think he appre-ciated my candor. But he did not stop.

In time, after failed attempts at treatment, the partnership agreed to exclude this partner from the firm. Ultimately he died, I believe in part due to this illness. It took tremendous effort on our part to somehow deal with this problem. I now realize that it is best to try to avoid it in the first place by carefully screening who you hire and associate with, by limiting the use of alcohol in business settings, and by encouraging those who have an alcohol problem to get help, specifically by joining Alcoholics Anonymous. For my part, in view of the negative impact alcohol has had on society in general through such things as drunk drivers, broken homes, increased medical costs, and catastrophic illnesses, I have chosen to not drink at all.

Just to put matters in perspective, however, I believe we all lead lives with some sort of vice or addiction at the door. It could be alcohol, it could be drugs, it could be food, or even manic exercise. The point is to stay balanced and keep your vices at bay, preventing them from affecting your professional or personal life.

THE POWER OF EFFECTIVE COMMUNICATION

*The more we elaborate our means of communication,
the less we communicate.*

–J.B. Priestly, *Televiewing, Thoughts from the Wilderness* (1957)

Too many of us take the wonder of communication for granted. Take this moment, for example. I make some marks on a piece of paper, which become symbols, and which, when placed before your eyes, register a meaning in your brain, essentially transferring a thought from my mind to yours. Isn't that absolutely amazing?

Equally amazing is your ability to emit air through your vocal cords while bringing them to vibration, resulting in the creation of a sound, which passes through the air. As that sound enters my ears, it hits my eardrums in a way that results in passing a signal to my brain, which registers your idea in my mind! Isn't that also amazing?

When we communicate, we use three levels of cognition: the sensory level, the perceptual level, and the conceptual level. Unfortunately, because we take being able to communicate for granted, few of us bother to hone our skills to ensure we are effective with our communication. In this chapter, I want to highlight some areas that commonly require some sharpening.

Being Concise

In his book *An American in the Gulag,* Alexander Dolgun tells a story that illustrates the importance of conciseness in communication. Following a period of liberalization after Stalin's death in the former Soviet Union, appeals to higher authorities in Moscow by innocent political prisoners in the camps of the gulag were entered thick and fast. One elderly Jewish man from Smolinsk wrote an appeal every week, always to the same address. After 12 weeks, he had received no reply. So, using what little money he had, he asked and got permission to send a cablegram to Moscow. The cable consisted of one word: "Nu?" (In English, "Well?")

That man understood how to be concise!

Conciseness literally means getting to the point. Here is a simple suggestion you can follow that will help you be more concise. In the old days, when people sent telegrams, they had to pay for each word. The longer the message, the more costly the telegram, so unless you were rich, you had to learn to convey a lot of information in a concise fashion. When you are preparing your remarks, letters, or any other form of communication, act like you have to pay for using each word. This will help you cut out a lot of frivolous and repetitive information.

I am reminded of a good story regarding the use of shorthand in telegrams that illustrates how to be concise. People were constantly asking film actor Cary Grant's agent how old the actor was, to the point of annoyance. One day, after seeing a telegram from a magazine editor to his agent asking "How old Cary Grant?" Grant responded with a telegram saying, "Old Cary Grant fine. How you?"

How Communication Affects Us

Even if you are concise, good communication always depends on the ability of the other party to interpret what you say. This is best illustrated by the experience of George Campbell, as related by Napoleon Hill and W. Clement Stone in their book *Success Through a Positive Mental Attitude.* Born with bilateral congenital cataracts,

George Campbell, like Helen Keller, lived in a world of darkness until the moment medicine finally developed a procedure to enable him to see. When he first opened his eyes after surgery, Campbell saw a flurry of light and a blur of color. His mind had not yet learned how to interpret his first sight of our world. Similar experiences have been reported by those who have had their hearing restored. The George Campbell story teaches us that effectiveness in communication depends completely on your mind's ability to interpret what it sees or hears. If we look at the process of communication, we realize that it is a process, which goes from the subjective stage to the objective stage and then back to the subjective stage.

For example, as I speak, the words I utter are subjective, dependent on the meaning and intention my mind ascribes to them. However, as soon as they leave my mouth, they take on an objective character. Their meaning is completely independent of anyone in this world. In fact, communication is one of the best sources of proof of the existence of objective reality. As the words enter your ears, these words become subjective again; their meaning depends on your mind's interpretation of them.

A Unique Experience

For me, one of the best examples of the effect of communication is illustrated by the following story.

In October 1990, I traveled with my 80-year-old mother to Kyiv, Ukraine, the land of her birth. Some 40 years earlier, she had fled Ukraine to come to Canada, and I was curious how she would react.

I loved my mother very much, but in order for you to appreciate this story, I have to point out that like many people her age, my mother was a little negative sometimes. You probably know the type. "This is no good," "That's wrong," etc. In fact, sometimes, when her complaints got out of hand, I joked with her by referring to her as the original "Mrs. No!"

On this trip, I was to be surprised by a remarkable transformation in her attitude. By sheer coincidence, while we were in Ukraine, a new museum to honor a famous opera singer was being opened.

The museum was dedicated to Salomea Krushelnytska, Ukraine's most famous opera star and the woman who helped the composer Puccini rescue his opera, *Madame Butterfly*, making it a success by singing the lead role in its debut. Salomea was my mother's aunt. In fact, my mother was named after her. When we heard of the event, we of course made it a point to attend.

As Ukraine was still under Communist control and travel was somewhat restricted, our attendance at this event was a novelty. When the public heard that the family of Salomea Krushelnytska was there, the visit turned into a national sensation. For the first time in her life, my mother became the focus of a national news media and an instant "public personality." A throng of some 200 people lined up to get her autograph. TV cameras juggled through the crowd to get a good view. Reporters noted her every word. The public seemed to hang on every syllable she uttered. In fact, she was so much a star on the occasion that people lined up to get *my* autograph simply because I was traveling with *her*!

That's where I witnessed the most astonishing transformation I have ever seen in my entire life. Suddenly, all my mother's negativity disappeared. She was energetic, buoyant, and electrifying. The pall of old age lifted from her shoulders. She walked out of that building a new woman who looked and acted 10 years younger! Right there I made two resolutions. First, I decided to pay closer attention when people speak because their speech is a direct channel to their self-image. Second, I resolved to get my mother's autograph!

It was amazing to watch my mother change when she realized that so many people wanted to know more about her family. The realization that what she had to say was of value changed the way she saw herself and the world around her. It is important to keep in mind that when you communicate, your words affect others. Your words can inspire and motivate someone, or tear a person down. You must be sure to use your words wisely. They are the most powerful tools you have to influence others.

Have Something Worthwhile to Say

Alexander Solzhenitsyn, who won the Nobel Prize in Literature, was once asked what made him a great writer. He said that in his life he had met many writers who were better than he was, but none of them experienced the Soviet gulag. His desire to relate the experience of life in Soviet concentration camps lifted his work to world stature and won him a Nobel Prize.

Not everything that comes to your mind is necessarily brilliant. Before sharing your ideas, you may need to do some work, undertake some research, or live with some hardships to accumulate some credentials. Put more simply, to be a great communicator, you must start by having something worthwhile to say.

Having something worthwhile to say is only part of being an effective speaker, however. We must not only have something worthwhile to say but also know how to present the material. Sometimes, it's not what you say, but how you say it.

Body Language and Voice

The extent to which body language and voice can affect communication was brought home to me during a business visit I made to Calgary, Alberta as a translator for two Kyiv oil and gas men who were trying to set up a joint venture in North America. One of the men, Dr. Melnichuk, spoke Ukrainian. The other, Professor Balakirov, spoke Russian. While I can generally speak both languages, my translating skills were soon to be severely tested.

Before entering the meeting, I briefed both gentlemen. I explained that the meeting was with 30 top oil and gas people in Calgary from the best firms. I continued by reminding them that this was North America, not the Soviet Union, and that here we expect our speakers to be brief, clear, and to the point. They assured me they understood!

The meeting opened well enough. Dr. Melnichuk spoke about the new opportunities for oil and gas in Ukraine, and then sat down.

Then it was Professor Balakirov's turn. You could see pretty soon after Professor Balakirov started that we were in trouble. His love for oil and gas clearly showed in his enthusiasm as he became submerged in details concerning enhanced oil recovery using an acidation process.

My ability to translate specialized Russian terminology was being taxed to the outer limits. Drawing an oil well on the blackboard, Professor Balakirov discussed inputs going in at the top and the outputs coming out at the bottom, audibly raising his voice in an effort to compensate for the loss of direct communication of all his words. Soon we realized a moment of truth: There were 30 people hopelessly adrift at sea with no anchor, and but one source of rescue—one cable connection to terra firma—my capacity to convey Professor Balakirov's meaning to the audience.

As I watched the professor enthusiastically raving about inputs at the top and outputs at the bottom, I wondered how in the world I would convey this to these busy corporate executives. Should I just stop and confess that I, too, was lost, that the complex terminology had baffled me, and that we were all, therefore, hopelessly adrift?

Finally, Professor Balakirov stopped and turned to me in the hope that I would then translate what he had just said. I got up, paused for a moment, smiled at the professor, and then proceeded in the simplest of terms to rave about the inputs at the top and the outputs at the bottom in the same manner that the professor had just displayed. Somehow, the meeting then proceeded to its conclusion.

It wasn't until late that night that I was to learn of the extraordinary success of our meeting. Even though I had an unlisted number, somehow, by the time I got home that night, my wife had received three phone calls from people at the meeting complimenting us on the great job we had done.

The moral of this story: Sometimes, it is more effective to convey the enthusiasm of the subject than the details!

The Power of a Single Word

One of the most extraordinary examples of the importance of communication was Helen Keller, who, at the age of two, was stricken with a disease that relegated her into a long night of darkness and silence by taking away her sight and hearing.

Surely, the most important moment in Helen Keller's life was the moment when, on April 5, 1887, her teacher showed her how to cross the threshold from darkness into light, from ignorance to knowledge, and from solitude to friendship. In her autobiography and other notes drawn together here in one passage, Helen Keller wrote about that moment:

> It happened at the well-house....As the cool stream washed over one hand she spelled into the other the word water, first slowly and then rapidly. I stood still, my whole attention fixed on the motion of her fingers. Suddenly I felt a misty consciousness, as of something forgotten—a thrill of returning thought; and somehow the mystery of language was revealed to me. I knew then that w-a-t-e-r meant that wonderful cool something that was flowing over my hand. That living word awakened my soul, gave it light, hope, and joy, and set it free....I reached out eagerly...begging for new words to identify whatever objects I touched. Spark after spark of meaning flowed from hand to hand and, miraculously, affection was born.

The Value of Communication

In his book *An American in the Gulag,* Alexander Dolgun relates his experience of 10 years' incarceration in Soviet concentration camps. The prisoners in those camps used a Russian prison tapping code as an elaborate form of communication, which was forbidden. This prisoners' Morse code was devised in the Tsarist era and passed on from prisoner to prisoner. But even those who had not read about it or learned it from others sometimes figured it out by listening to other prisoners tapping the alphabet over and over again together with one or two simple questions in the hopes that the prisoner might catch on.

In one passage, Dolgun relates his efforts to learn the tapping code that he encountered while he was sitting in his cell separated from other inmates by walls. He writes about the tapping code of another inmate:

> Why did he persist every night with the arithmetic lesson? 1–1, 1–2, 1–3, and so on to 1–6 until the pattern was completed with 5–6…Wait a minute! If you leave out the "hard" sign, you could say that the Russian alphabet has thirty letters. Five rows of six letters…The whole alphabet! My hands were shaking with excitement…I checked out the well remembered message: 2–4, 3–6, 3–2,…1–3, 5–2 K T O V Y "Ktovy?"—Who are you?
>
> Oh, God! A pure rush of love in my chest for a man who has been asking me for three months now who I am…Quick. piece out the numbers for Alexander Dolgun.

A similar story is told by Captain Jerry Coffee. Captain Coffee was shot down in an airplane above Vietnam when he was on a reconnaissance mission and ended up in a Vietnamese prison. In his book *Beyond Survival*, he writes, "Jerry, the tap code is our only dependable link to one another." This is in reference to another inmate telling him about the tap code.

> Somewhere on the walls of your cell you will probably find a little square matrix with twenty-five letters of the alphabet; five rows of five letters each, one row on top of the other. We leave out the letter K because we can use a C for the same sound most of the time.
>
> My mind was scanning back across the letters on the walls of the cells I had been in. Those damn little alphabet things had driven me bonkers, trying to figure them out. Now the mystery was about to be over. The first five letters, A through E, comprised the top row. Then came F through J in the second row, and so on. The rows were numbered top to bottom and the columns were numbered left to right. The faceless whisper from across the dim passageway continued. If you want to communicate the letter A to the man on the other side of the wall, you tap once for the row and once for the column. So A is one and one. If you want B, tap once for the row and twice for the column. B is one and two. For F, tap twice for the row and once for the column, so F is two and one. Thump! Thump! Thump! The same guard

re-entered the cell block. He was suspicious. There would be no more talking today. It became apparent my first communication lesson was over, but I would soon realize that Risner had provided the single most important lesson of my POW life.

These experiences point out the importance and value of communication in our lives. Through communication we achieve a sense of communion with each other—a closeness otherwise unattainable. The illustrations demonstrate that the value of this exchange is so great that men and women are prepared to go to extraordinary lengths to maintain it, whatever the setting, and even at the risk of death itself.

To summarize, effective communication requires mutual effort—yours and mine. It is a skill that must be mastered. Effective communication is a direct channel to high self-esteem. To be an effective communicator, you must have something worthwhile to say. How you say something is as important as what you say. We need to understand the value of human communication and the need to be clear in what we say and write. Communication is important to adding meaning and purpose to our lives. With one word, for example, Helen Keller was able to make the leap from darkness to light, and, thereafter, to a life full of hope and joy. If that is the power of communication, imagine the potential good communication can have in your life!

Seven Secrets to Improve Your Presentation Skills

Speak not but what may benefit others or yourself;
avoid trifling conversation.

—Ben Franklin (1798)

Not long ago, in Los Angeles, a chemical plant caught on fire. The fire department was called, but the firefighters could do very little because the blaze was out of control. As they stood in front of the factory, the owner rushed over and cried out, "Please help me save this factory! It's my life!" But there was nothing the firefighters could do. The owner then shouted out, "I'll give $50,000 to anyone who will go into that blaze and put that fire out." Nobody moved.

Just then, a siren sounded, and the Silver Fox Retired Fireman's Brigade truck burst through the crowd, driving right into the center of the blaze. Within a few minutes, the fire began to go out. Before long, there was nothing left but smoke. As the firefighters streamed out of the building, the owner was obviously elated. He ran up to the first man, handed him a check, and asked, "So what are you going to do with the money?"

The fireman answered, "Well, the first thing we are going to do is take the truck in to fix the brakes."

That story reminds us of how important it is to look after the basics. Whether you are talking about firefighting or about giving a presentation, the basics can make a big difference. Too many presenters—even the most professional among us—overlook the fundamentals of speaking. Time and again, they neglect the basics as if they did not matter. That is why I call these basics "secrets"—they are largely overlooked or forgotten by so many.

Over the course of my career, I would estimate that I have given more than 3,000 presentations and observed more than 5,000 others. This chapter summarizes what I have learned from these presentations. Learning the lessons contained in this chapter cost me countless hours of study, considerable effort, and thousands of dollars. I offer them to you here in the hope that they may help you in enhancing your presentation skills, and in the process, make life for all of us more enjoyable. I share this information not so much as an expert in making presentations, but more as a student of this wonderful art of communication. As a professional, you will without a doubt be called upon to make a presentation some time in your career. I share these remarks in the hope that you may find them useful when this happens.

In my career as an attorney, journalist, and speaker, I have seen the good, the bad, and the ugly. But one thing that I have learned is to recognize when I am in the presence of a great speaker. I know that I am hearing a great presentation when I get a chill down my spine as the speaker talks. Sometimes I feel the hair on my arms and at the back of my neck stand on end. I may even feel goose bumps run down my arms. I get so absorbed in the speaker's remarks that I forget about myself and my problems. I lose all track of time. I sense that the speaker's world is much larger than mine and I find myself lost in the speaker's world, even if only for a few minutes. As the presentation proceeds, I find myself hoping that the end is not near and that there is more that the speaker can give me. I suspect that at some point in your past, you, too, have experienced similar reactions to a great speaker.

If you have felt such sensations during a presentation, have you ever wondered how the speaker does it? What are the secrets that these great presenters use to make such an impact with their presentations? Let's take a look at some of them.

Secret 1: A Caring Attitude

I once spoke with a speaker who had just bombed on a program in front of a university audience. When I asked him what happened, the speaker answered, "That crowd is stupid and apathetic." I couldn't believe that, so I decided to talk to some members of the audience to find out what had transpired. I went up to the first man I saw and said, "You know, that last speaker was saying that this crowd is full of people who are stupid and apathetic. Do you think that's true?"

He said, "I don't know, and I don't care!"

They say it takes one to know one. Obviously, we as presenters cannot afford to be stupid. But even more important, we can't afford to not care.

As Ralph Smedley, founder of Toastmasters International, once pointed out, you can have one of two basic attitudes in your career and your relationships. When you are entering a boardroom, or indeed even your bedroom, there are only two basic approaches you can adopt. The first approach is, "Here I am!" The second approach is, "Ah, there you are!"

Only the second approach will win you the kind of respect reserved for professionals. All the great communicators of our time emphasize this point. Writer Ralph Waldo Emerson said, "Who you are speaks so loudly I can barely hear what you are saying." Mahatma Gandhi, one of India's greatest leaders, said, "Be an example of the kind of change you advocate for others." Cavett Robert, the founder of the National Speakers Association, used to say, "People don't care how much you know, until they know how much you care." And Zig Ziglar, one of the world's best speakers, often points out that people listen to radio station WIIFM—that is, "What's in it for me?" To be a powerful presenter, you must focus your attention on your audience, *not* on yourself.

Secret 2: The Structure of a Great Speech

Recently, three elderly men, all hard of hearing, were talking. The first one said, "Isn't it windy?"

The second man said, "Wednesday, I thought it was Thursday."

The third man said, "Thirsty? So am I. Let's have a drink!"

That story illustrates the problem of trying to communicate with someone who is preoccupied with his or her own concerns. The challenge of dealing with preoccupation is one of the first points covered by our second secret of powerful presentations—namely, remembering the structure of any great speech.

A great speech consists of four parts:
- The introduction
- The bridge
- The body
- The conclusion

Let's look at each one of these four parts in turn.

The Introduction

Because the introduction is probably the most important part of any presentation, it merits far more attention than the other parts. In the introduction, you must answer the question, "Why should I listen to you?"

As the speaker, you must capture the audience's attention. I am amazed how many speakers, including professionals, do not recognize that many people in the audience are preoccupied with their own problems and concerns. They are thinking:
- "Oh, I need to buy some milk on the way home today."
- "Gee, my son looked a little pale when he was leaving for school this morning. I hope he's not sick."

And so on.

Your challenge as a speaker is to break through that preoccupation. How do you do that?

My favorite way is to begin a speech by telling a story—particularly a personal story. The very fact that you are living on this Earth means that you have a unique point of view and an original story to tell. Use it! Besides, one good personal story is worth more than a thousand words of narrative. When we relate stories, especially childhood stories, we unlock emotions that have been sealed away in our memories. Stories enchant the audience by touching them at the subconscious level and drawing them into the presentation. Other methods are to recite a poem, to cite a startling statistic, or to make an outrageous remark. Humor also works well, but only if it is very good. How do you know it's good? The only way to know that is to tell the story a few times to your friends to make sure it evokes a hearty laugh. Finding such a joke takes time and effort. Not all jokes are good!

Really, any technique that will capture the audience's attention will do. Here are a couple additional ideas:

+ Start your remarks in the middle of things. For example, "He stood at the doorstep with a bloody knife in his hands as he rang the doorbell" is preferable to, "He picked up a bloody knife on the grass. Then he walked toward the house. He walked up the stairway. He then rang the doorbell, and waited for someone to answer."

+ Apologizing for your speech is one surefire way of destroying your presentation. Apologies for being late, for not having a prepared speech, for reading from a written text, or such other comments have no place in a powerful presentation.

Like a train that first connects with its caboose, and then pulls the caboose along to where it wants to go, you as a speaker must first meet the audience where it is before you can take it to where you want it to go. This may require you to stand at the podium surveying the audience, sometimes even for several minutes, waiting for it to calm down before you begin. Taking a few moments to connect with your audience before moving into the introduction of your speech helps you to set the proper timing for your remarks. Surveying your audience before you start puts you on the right track. Failing to connect can drive you right into the ditch. Only after you are sure you have a sense of the audience's mood should you begin to speak.

The Bridge

In the bridge, you must forge a bond with your audience. You must connect with your audience at the emotional level. You must answer the question, "Why should I care?" During the bridge, you'll find yourself using words like, "Imagine if you...," "What would you do...," or "Picture yourself doing...." These are tools you can use to bridge the gap between you and your audience—hence the term "bridge."

In his remarks to the National Speakers Association convention a few years ago, Joel Weldon underlined how important it is to use the word "you" as often as possible in the early parts of your speech. Weldon encouraged speakers to record their presentations and actually count the number of times they used the word "you" compared to the number of times they used "I" and "we." As Weldon pointed out, we are all selfish audience members. If the presenter is not speaking about us or our concerns, we are not interested.

Dealing with Self-Consciousness

Why is it that when giving a presentation you can't be the same ordinary person you are day in and day out? Why is it that when you get up before an audience, you are suddenly very conscious of your hands when, otherwise, they never come to mind? This self-consciousness effectively erects a shield between the speaker and the listener. The shield prevents the real self from coming out to make contact with the listeners. When we are self-conscious, by definition, we are not audience-conscious.

Some speakers may not be self-conscious but instead focus on the content of their remarks at the expense of losing touch with their audience. This, too, is a cardinal sin in presenting.

If you must get lost somewhere, instead of losing yourself in your self-consciousness or in your speaking notes, lose yourself in your audience.

The Body

In the body of the presentation, you must present the "meat and potatoes." The audience is wondering, "What is the point?" During the body of the presentation, you must answer this question.

During this section of your presentation, remember that no audience can remember more than three or four points. But don't fret: Just about every subject in the world can be packaged into three or four points. It is just a matter of working at it.

The Conclusion

In the conclusion, you must lay down a challenge for your audience. The question in the minds of your audience is, "So what?" You must assign them something to do as a result of your remarks. Tell them to write a letter, stand up and be counted, or remember the three or four points that you presented. But have them *do* something.

Regardless of how seasoned a speaker you are, giving a presentation is very much like riding a bucking bronco. No matter how prepared you are and how much experience you have, it is impossible to hang on every time.

To borrow a little wisdom from the legal profession, every time you make a presentation, you actually give *three* presentations:

÷ You give the presentation on the way to the speech.

÷ You give the presentation at the speech.

÷ You give the presentation on the way home from the speech.

Sometimes, when things don't go right, all you can do is console yourself with thoughts like these.

Secret 3: Organizing a Powerful Presentation

A few months ago, I was driving on a highway in Alberta, Canada in the dark. It was snowing heavily, and blizzard winds made it almost impossible to see the road ahead. I was getting a little alarmed, but just then I saw a snowplow.

I remembered some advice my father once gave me: If you are ever caught in a snowstorm and see a snowplow, you should follow it to safety. So I started following the snowplow. After a while, it stopped. The driver got out and came over to talk to me. He asked me what I thought I was doing. I told him about my father's advice. He said, "Well, okay, but we've finished Wal-Mart and now we are going to go clear the Safeway parking lot."

That is a little story about how, if you just do what someone else is doing, you might end up going in circles. And it introduces the next theme of my remarks—namely, how to organize a powerful presentation so you can reach your goal.

NOTE: The approach that I am going to suggest is only one approach. It may not work for you. You may find that only parts are suitable to your style. It is offered only as one method of preparing a presentation. You may wish to try it or a variation of it. All I can say in favor of this method is that many speakers with whom I have shared this method agree that it is a good one.

One of the best ways to illustrate how to prepare a good speech is to draw an analogy to making chicken soup. Imagine, if you will, that you have never made chicken soup before. How would you do it? The process you would follow is very similar to the process for preparing a powerful presentation.

The first step you would take to make chicken soup would be to list the ingredients. You would write down water, chicken, carrots, onions, salt, pepper, etc. In preparing a speech, you would take a similar approach. After choosing a topic, you might list a whole series of ideas that come to you over a period of days related to the topic. Or, if you are researching the topic, you would list the ideas that come to you from your research.

Next, in making soup, to help you remember what you need to buy, you might group the soup ingredients into subcategories. For example, you might list under vegetables, the onions, the carrots, the celery, etc. Under spices, you might put salt and pepper, etc. Similarly, in the case of the speech, you would attempt to group the various concepts that you have listed.

A good way of doing this is as follows:

1. List each concept on a separate sticky note or index card.
2. Lay out the sticky notes or index cards in front of you on a table.
3. Organize the sticky notes or index cards in a series of groups.
4. Organize the groups into some sort of a sequence.

NOTE: This is an elementary form of storyboarding originated by Walt Disney at Disney Studios.

Once you have organized the ingredients for your soup, it is time to prep them. You have to peel the onions, the carrots, the celery, etc. In the case of a speech, once the ideas have been organized in a proper order, it is time to develop them. I suggest you either type out your ideas or write them out in longhand. This process clarifies your thinking. It crystallizes your vague ideas into concrete concepts. It removes the ambiguities from your presentation.

Once you have prepped the ingredients you want for your soup, you set the rest aside. Similarly, when you have written out and polished your ideas, it is time to dispense with your written notes and work from your concepts. The key here is not to recount your presentation word for word, but rather to recall key concepts and state them in your own words—albeit not the same words contained in your written out and polished ideas. It is time to single out keywords in each paragraph that will help you remember the ideas that are there. You may want to use a highlighter to single out a few words from each paragraph and commit them to memory.

You might make adjustments before serving your soup by adding an extra pinch of salt or a bit more pepper, etc. Likewise, with your speech, you can make adjustments as needed. To decide where, you need to practice. Practice your presentation orally over and over again. Practice it on the way to work in the car, in the shower, while you are jogging, and on the way to your meeting. It is important to actually speak the words out loud as part of your practice to surmount rough spots, introduce effective pauses to underline important points, and discover awkward phrasing that needs adjusting.

Concentrate on the introduction and the conclusion in particular. Make sure you have them down solid.

Finally, you are ready to make your presentation. Enjoy! Remember, like making chicken soup, speech-making gets better the more times you do it.

Secret 4: It's Not What You Say, It's What Is Understood That Matters

A new pastor arrived at the church on his first Sunday. He was somewhat disappointed to find that there was only one farmer sitting there when he arrived. He went to the farmer and said, "I don't know what to do. I've prepared a sermon, but I don't know whether I should give it or not since you are the only person in church."

The farmer said, "Well sir, I don't know anything about preaching, but I do know when it's feeding time, even if only one cow shows up, I still feed the animal." The pastor then resolved to give the entire sermon. He spoke for just short of an hour. When he finished, he went to the farmer to ask how he had done. The farmer said, "I don't know much about preaching, but I do know that when only one cow shows up at feeding time, I don't feed it the whole load."

Feeding the audience the whole load is one of the biggest mistakes that speakers make. Very often, even experienced speakers will try to compact a one-hour presentation into 15 minutes. Just like you can't swallow an entire turkey dinner in one gulp, it is impossible for an audience to digest a one-hour presentation in a few minutes. Presenting ideas too quickly, usually to cover too much content in too little time, is perhaps the most common mistake made by speakers. Slow down. Use pauses between ideas to give the audience a chance to catch up. Like a glass that can only contain so much water before it spills over, an audience can only absorb so much information in a certain period of time before it becomes overloaded. The objective is not to say everything you want to say but for the audience to retain everything you want them to retain.

Secret 5: Understanding How Your Audience Thinks and Feels

As leading psychologist Nathaniel Branden points out, communication involves several levels of experience. Drawing an analogy to someone playing a musical instrument helps to explain this concept.

Imagine someone is sitting in the corner of your room playing a violin. As the sound carries across the room, your ears register it as sensory data. In other words, you hear sound. Seemingly automatically, as the sound enters your ears, it is converted into precepts. At the perceptual level of consciousness, you perceive musical notes. Then, through a series of abstractions and using your willpower to concentrate on what you hear, you arrive at the conceptual level of thinking. You discern a pattern of musical notes, a particular song. Finally, at the interpretative level, as the music touches your emotions, you respond with your subjective feelings. If the music is a funeral march, you feel sad. If the music is an upbeat waltz, you feel happy. (See Table 1.)

Table 1 Levels of Audience Connection (Experiential Analysis)

Input	Mechanism	Experiential Level
Sound	Ears	Sensory
Sensory	Mind	Perceptual
Precept	Will	Conceptual
Concept	Emotions	Feelings

© Andy J. Semotiuk, 2013

The business world operates with a very similar gradation of understanding. At its most primitive level, we find data. When examined by the human mind, data becomes information. When information is studied, it becomes knowledge. As knowledge is interpreted by the human brain and placed in the context of experience, it is reduced to its essence and becomes wisdom. (See Table 2.)

Table 2 Gradation of Understanding in the Business World

Input	Mechanism	Result
Data	Mind	Information
Information	Study (will)	Knowledge
Knowledge	Thought and experience	Wisdom

© Andy J. Semotiuk, 2013

Such explanations of the process of communication are useful because they give you a glimpse into the mind of your audience as they strive to comprehend your presentation. It is impossible to completely understand the process of communication without looking at it through the prism of the human need it satisfies.

At the primary level, there is informational communication. An illustration might be a man walking down the street, approaching another man, and asking, "Where is Union Station?" The second man says, "Go two blocks left and one block right and you will be there." This exchange is an informational exchange at the lowest level. The need being satisfied is the need to know, to be informed, and to inform others.

The next level of communication is the intellectual or transactional level. This is the level in which the business world operates. You can describe this level of communication as a meeting of the minds. This is the level of agreements. It is also the level of communication that might be found when you attend a seminar and listen to a teacher present ideas. The needs being satisfied are the need to understand the world we live in and the need to be understood.

The highest level of communication is the spiritual level. This is a level where there is not only a meeting of the minds but also a meeting of the hearts. This is the level where we achieve not just communication, but *true* communion with others. This is the communication between "soul mates." This level of communication addresses our need to know that our lives are not merely a series of random coincidences, but that we really matter and that our lives serve some higher purpose on this Earth. See Table 3.

Table 3 Levels of Audience Connection (Needs Analysis)

Communication Level	Characterized By	Needs Met
Informational	Exchange of information	To know, to be informed, to inform
Intellectual	Meeting of the minds	To understand, to be understood
Spiritual	Communion	To know our lives matter, to know we have a purpose

© Andy J. Semotiuk, 2013

In everyday life, of course, you have to communicate on all levels. It is impossible to lead life at only one level of communication.

Secret 6: Two Contenders

Part of your challenge as an effective speaker is to keep your audience's attention. To understand how to keep your audience's attention, you must understand the two contenders that vie for our attention:

- In the left corner, or left hemisphere of your brain, wearing pin-striped trunks and representing logic, reason, linear thinking, mathematics, and a methodological approach, is Mr. Organization.

- In the right corner, or the right hemisphere of your brain, wearing yellow and pink polka-dot trunks and representing color, imagination, music, integrative thinking, and a total systems viewpoint, is Mr. Creativity.

NOTE: If you are female, substitute Ms. Organization and Ms. Creativity. Also, if you are left-handed, the hemispheres are reversed, so that your left brain is your creative brain.

These two contenders are extremely selfish, and constantly vie for domination of your attention and focus. If either one is ignored for an extended period of time, it gets jealous and, after five or so minutes, seizes control of the mind. For example, if Mr. Creativity is ignored for some time, you'll suddenly find your mind out on the Florida Keys in a sailboat, or high up in the Rocky Mountains, skiing during the winter. It is then very hard to bring the mind back to the matters at hand.

However, there is a way to occupy both these mighty contenders while giving a presentation. If you have ever been to a county fair, you may have seen a game called "Whack-a-Mole," involving a padded mallet and some moles that pop up, which you have to hit with the mallet. Imagine having to hit Mr. Organization and Mr. Creativity over the head, alternately, one after the other like those moles. This is the method that can be used by a speaker to satisfy both the intellectual and emotional needs of his audience.

The precise formula is point-example-story, or point-example-anecdote, or point-example-joke, or point-example-vignette, and so on. Employing this method of presentation keeps both Mr. Organization and Mr. Creativity happy, and keeps your audience aware and alert as to what you are doing.

While it is important for a speaker to address both the intellectual and the emotional needs of his audience, it is my experience that most speakers pay far too little attention to the emotional side. Too often, motivation and attitude are neglected for the sake of "intellectual" content. In almost every speech delivered these days, Mr. Creativity is neglected by presenters.

Don't let that happen to you!

Secret 7: The Power of the Spoken Word

Two men were sitting in a bar in Boston. The first man asked the second, "So, where are you from?"

The second man answered, "Dublin."

The first man said, "Isn't that amazing, so am I. Where did you live in Dublin?"

The second man said, "On St. Patrick Street."

The first man said, "Well, isn't that a coincidence, so did I! So what high school did you go to?"

The second man replied, "St. Mary's High School."

The first man said, "Well that's just unbelievable. So did I!"

This conversation continued.

Meanwhile, another patron entered the bar, approached the bartender, and asked "What's new?"

The bartender replied, "Oh, nothing. Just that the O'Malley twins are drunk again."

It's amazing how many people repeat the same thing over and over again, even though they should know better. I can't tell you the number of times I have seen professional people get up before an audience and actually read a speech. It seems that so few people are aware that there is a profound difference between the written and the spoken word. Yet, they should know better.

Deepak Chopra, a leading American physician, says that we are all spiritual beings living a human experience. In other words, we are all soul men and women, so to speak. If he is right (and I believe he is), and if I want to touch you at the deepest level with my remarks, then the question is, how can I touch your soul?

Well, I don't know where your soul is in your body. But I do know that the closest place to your soul is your emotions. If I can touch your emotions, I can communicate with your spiritual essence. And the most direct channel to your emotions is your hearing. The ears—not the eyes—are the most direct channel to the emotions. If you are interested not just in communicating, but actually experiencing communion with your fellow human being, then you must focus on the hearing channel. When I communicate through your hearing channel, my ideas pass through the membrane of your emotions en route to your intellect. In the spoken word, we speak more directly from the heart. Our thoughts are not cleansed or edited. They are the rough chaff of spontaneity. We use contractions and tend to be more time-specific and concrete in our thinking.

When you employ the written word, you are using the audience's visual channel. Sometimes this is quite appropriate. But if your goal is to reach the highest level of communication with your audience and touch your audience at the spiritual level, then you must realize that by employing the visual channel, your ideas will be filtered. This is because they must pass through an intellectual membrane en route to your audience's emotions. When we write, we use a language far more polished, reasoned, refined, and precise than the spoken word. But, these polished words often become abstract if they do not speak to the audience's emotions. Also, when words reach the audience's intellectual membrane first, the audience tries to think over them. But, when words touch the audience's emotions directly, they feel them more immediately. It's like instant gratification.

I came to realize the importance of the spoken word early in my life by being raised by a mother who was hearing-impaired. At the age of two, my mother contracted spinal meningitis, which largely took away her hearing. At the age of 12, she contracted scarlet fever, and what little hearing was left was attacked. These dual illnesses presented my mother with a special challenge: to communicate in a world where hearing was critical. As a young child growing up, my role became increasingly to translate the world around us into language she could easily understand. Among the skills I had to develop to communicate effectively with her were conciseness, precision, meaningfulness, specificity, concreteness, accuracy, relevance, significance, impact, and usefulness.

I learned that these were the hallmarks that distinguished the master of the spoken word from the others. And I have found that these same skills are used by the champions of the spoken word today. They are learned through realizing their importance, by observing others, and by practice.

Those who appreciate these differences are the stellar communicators of our time. There are few of them, but each is worth his or her weight in gold. Such stellar communicators know the difference between effective communication and great communication. They know that effective communication is the accurate transfer of an idea from one mind to another. But great communication is the accurate transfer of a feeling from one heart to another. In the end, people may forget what you say and even how you said it. But people will always remember how you made them feel.

In this chapter, I have summarized seven of the key secrets of being an effective presenter. I've talked about your attitude and about the structure of a great presentation. I've touched on how to organize a speech, dealt with how your audience thinks and feels, introduced you to Mr. Organization and Ms. Creativity, and distinguished between the written and spoken word. You may be thinking that this is a significant investment to make for the sake of making an effective presentation. You may wonder why you should go to all the trouble. The answer is to be found in the following true story.

One day, Henri Matisse went to visit his friend Pierre Auguste Renoir while he was painting. As Matisse sat there, watching Renoir work, he noticed Renoir flinch from the arthritic pain that shot up his hand with each touch of the paintbrush on the canvas. Finally, Matisse couldn't stand it any longer. He asked, "If it's so painful, why do you persist in doing it?"

Renoir answered, "The pain passes, but the beauty remains forever."

The pain of preparing yourself as a speaker will pass, but if you follow the steps outlined here, the beauty of your presentations will remain engraved in the minds and hearts of your audiences forever.

Power Networking: How to Rise to the Top of Your Field—Fast!

First Impressions

You cannot judge a man till you know his whole story.

–Thomas Fuller (1732)

In the late 1960s, I was a student at the University of British Columbia in Vancouver, Canada. Back then, Robert Stanfield had just been elected leader of Canada's Progressive Conservative Party. As part of his first cross-Canada tour, he came to our campus. One of my friends invited me to a private reception at a professor's home where Robert Stanfield was the guest of honor. The living room had been cleared of all the furniture except for one table, which was stocked with coffee cups, a coffee urn, and some cream puffs. There was not an inch of space left on the table.

Most of the people in the house were in the kitchen, making it crowded and stuffy. I decided to make my way out into the living room to relax for a minute. We were all anxiously awaiting Robert Stanfield's arrival.

I poured myself a cup of coffee and took one of the cream puffs. There I was, sipping my coffee in one hand and munching on the cream puff in the other. Then the thought flashed through my mind that there really was no place to put down the coffee cup and saucer or the cream puff should I need to do so. No problem, I thought. There's nobody else around. Then the doorbell rang. The lady of the house opened the door and, sure enough, it was Robert Stanfield.

He walked right into the living room and approached me, since I was the only one in the room. As I watched him walk over, almost as if in slow motion, my mind was racing. I thought, "What am I going to do with this cream puff and coffee in order to shake his hand?" While watching him, I slowly slid the coffee cup to the edge of the saucer to make room for the cream puff, thus freeing my right hand to greet Robert Stanfield. However, I miscalculated. In the process of placing the cream puff on the saucer beside the coffee cup, it split, and half of it ended up under the saucer. The cream had no place to go except into my hand. I couldn't see this, of course, but I could feel the cream oozing its way into my hand.

Unfortunately, by then, the critical moment had arrived. The professor's wife introduced us and Robert Stanfield stood before me with outstretched hand. What could I do? I had cream on my hand, but I had to shake his, didn't I? So I did! The smile on his face turned to an expression of dismay. He turned around to walk away, reached into his pocket to grab his handkerchief, and wiped the cream off his hand. Obviously, I didn't make the kind of impression that I had hoped to make on Robert Stanfield. But, at least I made an impression.

I never met Robert Stanfield again. I doubt he remembered my face or name, but I sure remember him. In Hollywood, they say, "There is no such thing as a bad review as long as they spell your name right." But I'm not so sure. Hopefully, when you make a first impression with someone, it won't be with cream in your hand and a blush on your face. This chapter will help you in that regard.

Overview of Networking

Everyone knows the saying, "It's not what you know—it's who you know." In Hollywood, they say, "It's not who you can call, but who will take your call." We all need those "connections" to get what we want financially, culturally, and even socially. But how do you make those connections without being manipulative or "using" other people?

Over the course of my career as an attorney, I have dealt with more than 10,000 clients. When it comes to networking, I have seen the good, the bad, and the ugly. More recently, when I was Chairman of the Networking Committee of the Beverly Hills Bar Association for three years, I learned some exceptional networking techniques that I would like to share with you.

Some Networking Basics

Almost invariably, at every large meeting you attend, you are given a name tag. This begs the question, where should you put it? Well, I have the answer for you: Put it on your right lapel. When you shake hands with people you're meeting for the first time, that side of your body will be put forward, highlighting your name tag. Having your name tag in the right spot is also a signal to other savvy networkers that you know what you are doing.

When you enter a room and do not see anyone you know, you might have second thoughts about wading into the middle of the crowd. You face a moment of truth. Not all the troops inside you are marching in the same direction, so to speak. Some of the troops may even want to retreat. The best way to avoid such a moment is to be the first person at the reception. That way, people coming in must come to you. But sometimes that is not possible. Sometimes, you have to enter a room full of strangers. It is awkward, but you just need to charge ahead. Approach the first person you see. Force yourself to get over that first introduction; it gets easier after that. The rewards are worth it.

When coming up to a new person, you should smile and look him or her in the eye. Stretch out your right hand with the palm facing slightly upward. The arm should be stretched out, but not completely. Your fingers should be slightly bent. Your palm should be slightly arched. Pause with your outstretched hand for as long as necessary until the other person grabs it. You may be frozen for a couple of uncomfortable seconds until the other person realizes he or she should shake your hand. But it is just part of the game.

Your handshake should be firm—not like a dead fish. A firm handshake displays confidence and strength of character. It says, "I am not afraid of you and I am prepared to deal with you as my equal." If appropriate, you should lightly touch the other person on the upper arm with your other hand, which adds warmth to your embrace.

This is the most friendly, inviting, and non-threatening way to initiate a handshake and open a conversation.

Start the conversation by telling the other person your name. Say something like, "Hi. I'm Andy Semotiuk." Sometimes, you bump into people who should know your name but may have forgotten it. In these situations, you should make it a point to help them remember. Say something like, "Hi. Remember me? Andy Semotiuk?" Keep eye contact through the entire handshake as the other person acknowledges you and introduces himself or herself. If you can, try to recall for the other person where you met before.

There is a popular tendency to be evasive about one's last name. People sometimes simply use a first name in introductions, perhaps due to hardship in pronunciation or some discomfort with the last name. I recommend resisting this trend. There is a wealth of information associated with a person's name—particularly his or her last name. A person's name is the single closest thing to his or her identity—that is, spiritual identity, or the "you" that is really inside. By getting a person's full name, you are getting that person to reveal a lot to you.

By learning someone's full name, you may be able to decipher his or her ethnic origin, geographic origin, association with the rich and famous, and so on. A name can give you priceless clues about that person. Do not let these valuable insights get lost in your encounter.

Invariably, I find that my probing into last names is appreciated because it signals more than a casual interest in a person. Even when the name is difficult, butchered by most of the population, that name is close and dear to the person involved. So make it a point to get the other person's last name. A good way to ensure you get it is to hold onto the person's hand during your handshake until you can ask for his or her name and he or she gives it to you. As long as you are being reasonable, this leaves an added impression on your new friend.

One of the most glaring ways people fail to effectively network is to survey a room looking for important people to meet while pretending to talk to the person in front of them. You "use" a person when you fail to reciprocate his or her attention or when you treat that person as a means to an end rather than as a person meriting your consideration. The person right in front of you should be the focus of your total attention. Forget about the others; focus on that person. The rest of the room can wait. My experience says that by doing this, you actually attract attention to yourself, and other people in the room will often make their way toward you. While you may not meet all the "important" people there, you certainly will have some interesting conversations.

Creating an Emotional Rapport: Your Networking Goal

The purpose behind networking is to develop a lasting bond with the people you meet—to make a connection. The bond can be intellectual, physical, or emotional. All are valuable, but the strongest bonds are emotional. I am not talking about romantic bonds. I am talking about affection, friendship, and comradeship.

The key to developing emotional rapport during a one-to-one meeting is eye contact. To ensure you are focused, make it a point to note the color of the other person's eyes. Try to focus on the eye that is to your right as you look at the person. That eye is the most direct channel to the emotional center of the other person's being. It is directly connected to the right hemisphere of the brain. That is where the person's emotions are registered.

Steven Covey had it right when he said, "First seek to understand and only then to be understood." If you are interested in power networking, you should try to make the other person feel that you understand him or her. You do this by acknowledging the other person's value through interacting with him or her. You do this by reflecting the person's underlying emotions back to him or her for that short time when you are together. Also, you do it by completely submerging yourself in the other person's life. You try to see life through his or her eyes and from his or her perspective. Take a genuine interest in the other person and in what that person says. Ask the person questions and listen. Be sincere. This is one of the most powerful tools you can employ to connect with another human being.

At some stage, of course, you will feel the need to move on to meet other people. I've noticed in political circles that diplomats sometimes like to break off a conversation by telling their guests a funny story and leaving while the guests are laughing. If you can do that, then all the more power to you. I have not yet reached that level of sophistication. Sometimes you can introduce the person to someone else and, as their conversation picks up, excuse yourself.

For me, a good way to break off is to say something like, "Well, it was nice talking with you, but I need something to drink." Or, "Well, it's time for me to go to the washroom." Even more directly, you can simply say, "It was really nice to get to know you. I think I'll move along now." These techniques free you up for your next encounter.

If I were asked to provide a concise statement of my philosophy of networking, I would use the words of the great Zig Ziglar, who says, "You can get anything in life you want so long as you help enough other people get what they want." If you want to rise to the top in your field, help other people get what they want. Sooner or later, they will help you. It is simple and it is true.

SKILLED NEGOTIATION

The secret of negotiation is to harmonize the real interests of the parties concerned.

–François de Calliéres (1716)

Almost everything in life involves negotiation. Negotiation can be described as the process of searching out common ground between differing objectives held by various parties. Whether you are dealing with items like office space, rent, salaries, or partnership agreements, you need to know how to negotiate.

The purpose of any negotiation is not to clobber the other side, but to come to an agreement whereby both sides can be happy. Unlike war or sports, in negotiations, both sides should end up winning something—particularly when the negotiation results in a relationship forming that will require participation by both sides.

Research the Other Side and Prepare

A good place to start the negotiation process is to research the background of the other negotiator. Using search engines on the Internet, try to find out as much as possible about the other person. This knowledge will help build trust, which is a key ingredient in effective negotiation.

NOTE: Just because you're negotiating doesn't mean you have to become a hard piece of concrete. Effective negotiators are people who personalize the circumstances, smile, are friendly, and use the other person's name. Just because interests are clashing between the parties doesn't mean that all humanity has to be lost. On the other hand, excessive emotion is not a good idea, either. Negotiations are generally lost by the one who loses his cool.

In preparing for negotiations, it is wise to make a list of as many questions as possible that you might pose to the other side. It is also an excellent idea to prepare a written draft agreement along the lines of what you would like to see come out of the negotiation. My experience is that the negotiator who asks the most questions and has a clear idea of where he or she wants to take the discussion will be in control of the meeting. Yet the ultimate power you have as a negotiator is in your ability to get up and walk away if the situation is absolutely unreasonable.

The language used in negotiations is very important. It is critical to avoid subjective adjectives, such as generous (to whom?), fair (to whom?), reasonable (to whom?), and other such words. The notion is to be human, but not to use inflammatory language when dealing with the other side.

Seek Advice on Strategy

In the early 1980s, I represented a 14-year-old boy who was crossing an intersection on his bicycle when a car came through and crashed into him. The boy sustained serious brain injuries.

After commencing a legal action, I arranged settlement discussions with the insurer's attorney. In preparing for these settlement discussions, I carefully reviewed the entire circumstances in the file. I also decided to call Roger Dawson, whom I had met at a National Speakers Association convention. Dawson is a leading expert on negotiation and author of the book *How to Be a Power Negotiator.*

My quandary was how to best present the boy's injuries. I felt that if I brought the boy to the meeting, he would be a distraction, and because he was restless and young would not benefit the negotiations.

On the other hand, I also felt that the other side needed a visual reminder of the severity of the boy's injuries.

Dawson suggested that I bring the boy in at the beginning of the negotiations for a brief meeting with the attorney and the representative of the insurance company and then have him go home with his mother while I continued the negotiations. This was extraordinarily effective because it gave both the attorney on the other side as well as the insurer the opportunity to see first-hand how serious the accident was. The result was a very significant settlement on behalf of the boy. The point is that it helps to ask colleagues who are experts on negotiation how to best present a case.

Bargaining

In my experience, the opening demands of the parties are critical to the results of the negotiation. It is important to present what your case is all about and why it deserves the ultimate offer, highlighting the uncontrollable and potentially explosive issues of the matter to prompt the highest possible first offer. It is also important in opening negotiations to understand that, generally, he or she who comes out with the first figure loses. This is because we really don't know where in the universe the other side is with respect to this negotiation. You may often be surprised at the generosity of the starting point involved if you elicit the offer first from the other side.

I have often told my clients that their job in coming to a negotiation is to react to the offer put forward by the other side. If you have ever studied neuro-linguistic programming (NLP), you know that the physical posturing involved in a negotiation can be significant. I have had occasions when, in the course of meetings, I have told my clients to mimic the behavior of the other negotiator when he or she was making positive comments, but to cross their arms and sit back when the other negotiator was making negative comments. NLP researchers have discovered that we tend to like people who adopt the same postures as we do, even though on a conscious level we don't know why that is so. We tend not to identify with people who have postures different from ours.

In a professional situation, one of the first things to be negotiated with clients is the professional fee. Believe it or not, establishing exactly what the professional fee for services rendered will be and getting a commitment in kind is a *sine qua non* of commencing any professional work for a client. Every time I failed to establish my fee up front, I was always disappointed.

I learned this lesson from shrewd taxi drivers in Eastern Europe. These taxi drivers would invite me into their taxi and take me to distant locations without ever mentioning cost. It was only upon arriving at the location that I learned how exorbitant a fee they were charging me. This was a shock. And it was my mistake. I should have negotiated the price before I even stepped into the taxi.

I was always taught never to accept the first offer in a negotiation, and generally speaking that is my practice. However, much to my regret, I once employed this tactic with Peter Fairbrother, a dear friend and neighbor. Peter offered to sell me his used computer because he was buying a brand new one. Because we were friends, he offered me the computer at a very fair price. Having just been schooled in negotiation tactics, I came back with a counteroffer. This was a mistake, and it soured our relationship. I regretted it from that moment on, but it was too late. Sometimes you have to adjust the rules regarding negotiations to fit your circumstances, which unfortunately I failed to do in this instance.

Often, a good approach to negotiation when the other side puts an offer forward is to indicate that you are disappointed and that you had expected quite a bit more. Sometimes, when the offer is in fact substantially lower than what you hoped for, an effective tactic is to get up to leave, but then at the last minute ask, "Is that the best you can do?" This tends to elicit a more generous offer and puts you in a better place from which to start your bargaining.

A Good Example

One of the most instructive experiences I've had regarding negotiation involved my cousin, Alex Tyshovnytsky. Alex was a high-powered executive in the financial community until he passed away a few years ago.

One day, Alex agreed to help me buy a car for my son, Mark, in Los Angeles. When we went to the dealership, we identified the car in which we were interested. Before talking to the dealer, we agreed that we would bid only on this car and not on any others. We also agreed that we would not take a test drive until we had reached some agreement with respect to the price to be paid. This would save us time and help us avoid the dealer's tactic of trying to get us to fall in love with the car before we started negotiating. Finally, we agreed that Alex would be our spokesperson and nobody else would enter the fray.

We entered the dealer's office and sat down. Alex pointed out the car in which we were interested and asked for the price on that car. The dealer put forth a number—around $10,000 plus registration and certain other fees. I was ready to start negotiating with that figure, but Alex made it a point to become more specific. He pulled out a piece of paper and wrote down the number 10,000. He then asked, "Are there any other fees or charges?" The dealer said, "Well, I'm not sure of the amounts." Alex said, "Could you please find out the amounts?" So the dealer came back with specific amounts. There was a registration fee of $100, insurance of $50, taxes, etc.

Alex proceeded to identify every single item, listing it on the piece of paper, and then totaling it to find the ultimate price. Only then did he ask if this was the price of the car. The dealer, now somewhat squeamish, indicated it was. That was the starting position. Now that we knew exactly what the total cost was, we could bargain with the dealer to come up with a fair deal. We ultimately bought a car at a very reasonable price to everyone's satisfaction, especially my son Mark's.

The Weakest Link

Research shows that like a chain, any bargaining position is only as strong as its weakest link. As professionals, we have a tendency to try to pull together several arguments for a position. But this can be a mistake.

A bargainer will ask why we are taking a certain position. We will put forward our strongest argument. The argument may be conclusive. If that's the case, a clever bargainer will ask, "Well are there any other reasons?" We will probably advance one or two other reasons. The clever bargainer will be looking for a weak spot in those reasons. If he doesn't find one, he may ask, "Is that all?" Again, we may advance another argument.

What the clever bargainer is really looking for is one argument that he or she can totally trash. As soon as the bargainer finds it, that person will seize upon it and crush it. Having done so, the bargainer will have also effectively crushed our entire position.

The best way to avoid this scenario is to answer the invitation for further arguments with our own question: "Does that mean that you accept our strongest argument?"

Timing Counteroffers

The worst time to put forward a counteroffer is just after the other side has put forward its offer. This is because the other side is not interested in hearing a counteroffer, as they just invested a substantial amount of time in putting forward their offer. The way to respond in a situation like this is to ask questions to pinpoint the weaknesses of the offer being put forward. Again, questions are what control the discussions.

Labeling Conduct

In asking questions, it is effective to also label your conduct. By this I mean saying, "Can I ask you a question?" This effectively freezes the other side's conduct and forces them to address the question being asked. Similar labeling helps control how the meeting progresses.

Straddling the Gap

Once the initial positions have been put on the table, it is important to focus not on the positions but on the difference between the two positions, financially speaking. Try to minimize the difference and look for ways to bridge the gap.

When you are straddling the gap between two figures, as you make concessions, they should become increasingly smaller as you progress. This lets the other side know that you have been pushed nearly to your limit. It is also a good bargaining technique to insist that with each concession you make, the other side must respond with one of their own.

Chinese Negotiating Tactics

In the early 1980s, I traveled to China to negotiate a contract for an airplane factory in Beijing. We were dealing with a gigantic engineering company, and I was involved with a small airplane manufacturing group.

Two experiences stand out in the process of those negotiations. The first was that the relative values of the assets we were bringing to the table were more important in the international field than the actual values. For example, we had invested $75,000 in building a prototype for a small ultra-light airplane. In the discussions, the Chinese put forward a valuation of their factory at some several hundred thousand dollars. While we did not accept this value, we put forward the proposal that we *would* accept the value if they were prepared to accept that our airplane was worth $200,000. Oddly, the Chinese agreed. Absolute values were not as important as the negotiated values in the context of the agreement.

A further tactic used by the Chinese, which was very effective, was to substitute negotiators. The first negotiator would wear us down over the course of several hours, and just when we thought we were making progress, they would introduce a second negotiator as the first one left. The result was more grinding. They sought out as many concessions as possible. Ultimately, we were so frustrated that we just caved in. The tactic was very effective.

It is really important *not* to disclose information to the other side that they can use against you. For example, the Chinese negotiators knew which day our flights were leaving, and were aware that we had made a significant investment of our time, effort, and finances to travel to China. They cleverly took advantage of this situation by delaying the negotiations to the last minute. Because we were pressed for time and had invested significant amounts to get there, we were more inclined to make unnecessary concessions. A wiser move would have been not to disclose the time limit.

Similarly, in respect to items that you are promising, it is always wise to estimate that it will take longer to conclude than you think it will, and that it will be more expensive than you expect it to be. In one real-estate negotiation in which I participated, the organizer of a limited partnership raised some $20,000 more than the $100,000 that he needed because he wanted to be sure that he would not have to make a second cash call on the partners. This was a wise move.

All this leads to the conclusion that 80 percent of the money to be made in negotiation is going to be made in the last 20 percent of the time. Smart negotiators will bear this in mind when they enter their negotiations. Indeed, it is critical to understand that you will never make more money in negotiating than in the final moments of bargaining. These final moments are critical.

A Professional Can Help Sometimes

Sometimes, when matters are important to you and the amounts are large, it's wise to engage a professional negotiator to negotiate the transaction for you. By doing so, you remove any emotional involvement in the transaction. Moreover, because the person is a professional, he or she is likely to do a better job for you than you would do yourself.

I did this when negotiating for a law office facility at West Edmonton Mall, back then the largest indoor shopping mall in the world. My friend, Nick Senenko, who was an architect as well as a negotiator, negotiated an office facility for me at a price substantially lower than

I could have ever negotiated myself. Nick understood all the elements of a lease, something that would have taken me a long time to figure out at the time.

Wrapping Up

It's important not to leave any details on the table. Vagueness is the Achilles' heel of effective negotiations. It's important to spell out every single point. Get everything down into a memorandum of agreement while everyone is present. Sign that, and then put it in legal form. Make sure you are the one who is concluding everything in legal form, drawing up the agreement. There are a lot of loose ends that can be specified in your favor at that moment.

It is always helpful in the final stages of a negotiation to make a small concession that may be largely meaningless but shows some element of good will. The important thing about making such a concession is the timing—it must come at the very end. Further, once the agreement is signed, it is important for you to give more than what is promised. This, too, buys good will as well as other opportunities to flourish both with this client and with others.

GETTING WHAT YOU DON'T WANT OUT OF YOUR LIFE

Adversity reveals and shapes character.

–Anonymous

Most people recognize the symbol of justice: a blindfolded woman holding a sword in one hand and a pair of scales in the other. Actually, this is the Roman goddess Justicia, who is blindfolded to symbolize impartiality. Unable to see either party in a dispute, she must decide by hearing their arguments. The sword represents just punishment for transgressions of the law, which Justicia determines by weighing the evidence on her scales of justice. I have a similar pair of scales in my office because I am in the legal business. But the scales serve another valuable purpose: They remind me about how I made some great improvements in my life. The scales remind me that great changes are made in increments—they are not instant.

Take, for example, quitting smoking—one of my greatest challenges. If you can imagine smoking as a heavy weight placed on the negative side of the scales, you have a good picture of where I started in addressing this problem. After 10 years, this habit had a solid grip on me. The key to changing this habit was to accumulate enough positive counterweights to tip the scale in favor of a healthier lifestyle. It wasn't easy. In fact, it was the hardest thing I had ever done in my life. It required introspection—learning that for me, moderation was more difficult than quitting cold turkey. It required commitment to a new way of living each day. It required talking with other people who had quit, seeking reassurance. It required strength of resolve and character. All these steps added more counterweights on the scale. Finally, I set a deadline and marshaled all the willpower within me to do it. The scales tipped!

I tipped the scales again when I had to lose 40 pounds. Imagine years of poor eating habits and indulgences placed on one side of the scales. My first step was to acknowledge that I was indeed fat, not just slightly overweight. I had to acknowledge the problem—namely, that I looked like the Pillsbury doughboy. Too many donuts! I started to read books on diet, exercise, and health. I then made daily exercise a higher priority than anything else by running five times a week. From Monday morning to Friday evening, I strictly regulated my food intake. I identified four or five key foods that were causing major problems in my diet: peanuts, chips and other packaged snacks, sweets, ice cream, and cheese. I cut these out completely and turned to more wholesome, less-fattening alternatives, which I found at health-food stores. On weekends, I rewarded myself for my successes by relaxing my diet within reason or by attending some special event like a football game. Step by step, I put counterweights on the scales until they tipped again.

Yes, as the scales tipped, I experienced some glorious moments. But it would be wrong to view my accomplishments only as snapshots of these moments that tipped the scales. That would be like playing tennis with your eye on the scoreboard instead of on the ball. In business, it would be like focusing on how much someone can spend without asking how he or she made the money.

The point is to become the kind of person who can pay the price to succeed, not just to be a success. It is the difference between the authentic achiever and the imposter.

How to Put the Fun Back into Your Work

In the late 1980s, I was struck by something that I experienced as an attorney. In many ways, I was confronted with the negative aspects of life. I was concerned with the resolution of conflicts, the dissolution of relationships, the conclusion of unsuccessful businesses, the identification of potential hazards for parties entering commercial transactions, etc. I hasten to add that there are positive aspects to practicing law as well. But in my case, I concluded I was spending too much of my time on the down side of life.

I was not happy with those aspects of practicing law that forced me into situations where I was dealing with coercion, vindictiveness, and the darker passions. I decided to turn myself around. I turned my attention away from those dark elements in life.

Here is what I did: I took a five-step process to turn my career around and make it more satisfying and more meaningful to me. I figured this process out by reading various books on success. I believe people in any profession can use this same process to turn themselves around if they are unhappy in their situation.

Step One

The first thing I did was to define for myself in black and white, on paper, what I liked about my job and what I disliked about it. I then made it a point to focus my attention and activities more in the area of those things that I liked. For example, I enjoy meeting people. I like writing. I enjoy working on computers. I get pleasure from going to meetings. I decided to pay more attention to these areas. I decided, for example, to avoid vicious family fights between husbands and wives over children. I decided to avoid highly emotional conflicts between clients. Instead, I tried to concentrate on what I liked in my job.

Step Two

The second thing I decided was to deal only with clients who I defined as "good people." I decided purposefully to screen the people who walked through my door and to decide which people I was going to deal with and which people I was not going to deal with. I decided that I was at a point in my career where I could select my clients rather than have my clients select me as their attorney.

Step Three

The next thing that I did was to decide to keep my life in better perspective. I imagined my life as a huge circle with a black dot in the middle. The black dot represented everything that was bad in my life. The huge circle represented my life in general. I got this from the book *How to Stop Worrying and Start Living* by Dale Carnegie. As discussed in earlier in this book, Carnegie asserted that most people spend too much time focusing on that little black dot that represents what is wrong in their lives and too little time on the larger circle, or what is good in their lives. I, too, was guilty of this transgression. Too often, I would beat myself up by compulsively worrying about my problems.

For example, I could not keep my financial affairs in a proper perspective. Instead of adopting the right perspective, I would fret and worry about my circumstances at the moment. This would amplify my anxieties by emotionally charging the problem, which already was spiraling out of control.

What I failed to understand was that we view every problem through the prism of a time frame. Invariably, when a problem seems out of control, it is because we have chosen to view it from the worst possible perspective. This was the case with my financial woes. You can look at a problem from the viewpoint of a week, a month, a year, or a lifetime. Since time frames are totally arbitrary, they are up to you. To address your problems effectively, you should choose those time vantage points that most empower you to act.

By consciously choosing to view my financial situation in a proper time frame, by seeing the problem in the context of what I would earn over the course of a whole year, I drained its emotional juices and empowered myself to deal with it. The result was I could sleep at night again.

Step Four

Step four was to occasionally make a list of all those worries or concerns that were tormenting me. I usually did this in the early hours in the morning when I could not sleep due to events that seemed to be disturbing my otherwise peaceful life. I found that by writing out my concerns, by listing them on a piece of paper, I could "flush" out my worries from my system and effectively "cleanse" my mind to regain a sense of calm and control. My mind would thus unburden itself of its excess baggage.

Step Five

Finally, I realized it is useless to lament what should be, what could be, and how I should have achieved this or that goal. What is preferable is to accept the hand that you have been dealt and to play that hand in the best way possible. Instead of regretting what you do not have, do the best you can with what you *do* have.

You may be thinking that you don't want any problems in your life. As Dr. Norman Vincent Peale pointed out, however, the only people who don't have problems are people who are buried in the cemetery. Living is all about dealing with problems. Just get used to the fact you will always be facing some sort of problem as long as you are alive.

When your whole world seems to be caving in on you, it isn't easy to stay focused on what is really important—solving the problem. A successful professional trains himself or herself to find the problem and then selects the proper tool to fix it. Clearly define what is wrong and what is *not* wrong. Break the problem down into its component parts and address them one by one according to their priority. These problem-solving skills must become a habit—an intrinsic part of your nature.

The five points I mentioned: to focus on what I like, to deal with good people, to keep a proper perspective, to make a list of my worries to flush them from my mind, and to play the hand that I have been dealt, helped me turn my practice and my career around. Of course, my problems did not just go away. But, by applying these disciplines and keeping my problems in perspective, I have made my life much more enjoyable.

Never Quit

*Never give in—never, never, never, never, in nothing great or small,
large or petty, never give in except to convictions of honor and good sense.
Never yield to force; never yield to the apparently
overwhelming might of the enemy.*

–Winston Churchill

Many years ago—on December 10, 1958, to be exact—I watched a
boxing match between Archie Moore, the light-heavyweight champion of the world, and Yvon Durelle, the Canadian champion and
contender for the world crown. As I watched, I knew I was witness-
ing something important. It was only decades later, however, after I
reflected on the match, that I really grasped the lesson of that
evening.

I had never really liked boxing as a sport. It was always too coarse
and brutal. Yet that night, I sat glued to my black-and-white television set, mesmerized by the contest between these two men. The
contrast between the two fighters could not have been greater.
Durelle, the challenger, was a 29-year-old white French Canadian
fisherman from Baie St. Anne, New Brunswick. He showed up at
weigh-ins in a ski sweater and old work pants. Bewildered by all the
media attention, he was obviously the underdog, and the media
clearly made a big deal about this, his one big chance to achieve
world stature. But it was Moore, an African-American in his 40s
who came from San Diego, California, who would teach us all a great

lesson that night. With more than 200 career fights and 126 knock-outs, Moore had earned international attention as a suave cosmopolitan who showed up at weigh-ins in a midnight blue tuxedo with a black silver-tipped cane. The goatee that adorned his chin emphasized his worldliness and international stature.

When the fight started that night, however, the two men entered the ring and started as equals. Right from the beginning, Moore was in trouble. In the first round, Moore hit the canvas three times. Each time, the crowd was brought to its feet, sensing imminent doom. Each time, Moore seemed dazed and groggy. But each time, he somehow managed to get back up on his feet. Incredibly, Archie Moore survived that first devastating round.

In the fifth round, disaster struck Moore once again. Again, he hit the canvas. Again, the crowd was brought to its feet, sensing the end was near. Again, the champion looked dazed and groggy. But again, as we all counted, the champion again got up on his feet and back into the fight.

Now it was time for the master to teach his pupil a few things. In the seventh round, Durelle was floored for a two count. A momentary lapse, we thought. Then, in the 10th round, the challenger was brought to his knees by a six-punch barrage, but was saved by the bell that ended the round.

The end was near. It came 49 seconds into the 11th round. By then, Durelle had been knocked down twice. He didn't get up the second time. The fight was over. Archie Moore became the "KO King" with his record 127th knockout victory. Moore had come back from four knock downs to successfully defend his world title.

In the days that followed that fight, people talked about how it was the greatest test of human endurance they had ever seen. But it was even more than that: It was a test of character. Each man was called upon to summon everything he could find from deep inside to help him withstand the challenge. Each man was knocked down, but only the champion refused to stay down.

Life, like that fight, is also a test of character. Each day, we face challenges, and sooner or later we will face setbacks. Setbacks such as a death in the family, an illness, the loss of a job, a divorce, or a business failure are part of the human experience.

When you are faced with a personal setback, don't give up. That was the message Archie Moore communicated to us in that fight on December 10th, 1958. His example taught us that a true champion is someone who, when he finds himself lying on the canvas, drained of all his energy, summons whatever courage and strength it takes to get back on his feet and back into the fight. Moore taught us that you must find the determination, you must find the persistence, you must find the stamina to continue on. Never quit! Never quit! Never quit!

The Value of a Higher Purpose

He conquers who endures.

–Persius

I don't think you need this book to inform you that life is not always easy. In the face of extraordinary hardships, I have always been inspired by the great heroism often displayed by the people involved.

I believe the essence of great character and strong values can be discerned from how people behave in extreme conditions, such as inmates in concentration camps. Studying such situations helps clarify your own beliefs and strengthens you for the challenges life may send your way.

There is little doubt that much can be learned from reading stories such as these. But their impact on you and your life will depend on you. If you merely read them, they will be of little value to you. But if you accept them with an open heart, they can inspire you to accomplish great things—to rise to your calling and become the great person you were intended to be.

This chapter recounts one such true story about a client of mine, shared with his permission.

Arrival at Auschwitz

Finally, the train stopped. After four days of starvation and thirst, sealed and wired shut in stench and filth with 120 other prisoners in a boxcar with no toilets or water, John Lahola was apprehensive but relieved that his uncertain journey was over. For four days and nights, the fearful occupants had recited prayers in Polish as they anxiously awaited their fate. It did not matter that most of them were Jews and Ukrainians—in Polish prayer, they all found common solace.

Four days earlier, the prisoners had been forcibly taken from Gestapo headquarters in Nazi-occupied Lviw and loaded on this train bound for an unknown destination. Now, as the SS guards flung open the boxcar doors, a welcome burst of fresh air flooded the compartment. It also revealed to the prisoners where they had arrived: Auschwitz.

It had been more than three months since John Lahola was arrested for his support of the Ukrainian partisan underground resistance to the Nazi occupation of Ukraine. For a split second, as the Gestapo placed him under arrest in Lviw, Lahola had caught a glimpse of his mother across the street. As John sought to wave goodbye, he was struck over the head by the butt of a soldier's gun. John did not know then that in that place, at that moment, and in that manner, he was parting from his mother forever. Thus began the relentless march of events that ended here, with these fellow prisoners, in this place, the most notorious death camp of Nazi Germany.

"Never shall I forget that night, the first night in camp, that turned my life into one long night, seven times sealed," wrote author Elie Wiesel in his heartbreaking book, *Night*, about his time as an inmate at Auschwitz. Like John Lahola and countless other prisoners who experienced the horror of Auschwitz, Wiesel was forever tormented by his memories of the camp.

In *Night*, Wiesel writes:

> Never shall I forget the smoke. Never shall I forget the small faces of the children whose bodies I saw transformed into smoke under a silent sky. Never shall I forget those flames that consumed my faith forever. Never shall I forget the nocturnal silence that

deprived me, for all eternity, of the desire to live. Never shall I forget those moments that murdered my God and my soul and turned my dreams to ashes. Never shall I forget those things, even were I condemned to live as long as God Himself. Never!

It was under these conditions that psychiatrist Victor Frankl, also a former Auschwitz inmate, was able to develop a deeper understanding of the human mind and the foundation of his theory of human survival. Frankl observed that while many inmates perished, some Auschwitz inmates managed to survive despite the hardships and privations. He asked, why? How did people like John Lahola manage to survive in such inhumane conditions?

In his book *Man's Search for Meaning,* Frankl states that the answer was to be found in the prisoner's attachment to some larger explanation of his or her existence—some higher purpose to his or her life.

According to the book and also a biography of the psychiatrist's life later written by Dr. C. George Boeree, Frankl hypothesized that the difference between those who perished and those who survived was to be found in the manner in which the inmates translated the meaning of their suffering to themselves. Those inmates who lived with a higher purpose in life were able to endure the hardships and sacrifices because they could be explained as necessary evils that had to be surmounted for the sake of the higher end. Those inmates who existed without a larger philosophical framework through which to interpret their suffering died. It was Frankl who quite rightly pointed out that one of our most deeply rooted needs is to believe that our life has meaning, that our setbacks and efforts to overcome them carry a significance apart from the mere events themselves, and that they fit into a bigger picture.

This knowledge armed Frankl with a weapon he could employ in helping fellow inmates. He knew that while an inmate could do absolutely nothing to avoid the extreme external events occurring around him from day to day in the camp, the inmate alone controlled how he or she would interpret the events and react to them. If the inmate could identify a "higher" purpose to his or her sufferings, this would serve as a key to the inmate's survival.

Whenever a fellow inmate would turn to Frankl exhibiting signs of depression or resignation, Frankl would ask the prisoner why he didn't just give up. Frankl would then intently listen to the prisoner's response, which would usually be something along the lines of, I would give up, but I have a wife, or a child, or maybe a political cause or religious belief, etc. Whatever the prisoner proffered in that moment, Frankl would seize upon it as the anchor to that inmate's continued survival. The prisoner's answer was really his reason for living and was a powerful key to the inmate's continued existence. If the inmate spoke of a wife, for example, Frankl would endeavor to direct all his comments and explanations for what was taking place toward that idea, linking everything to it and thus developing a whole rationale for the prisoner on why he must continue the struggle to survive.

In his own case, Frankl rationalized his suffering by focusing on his wife's beautiful hands. He told himself he must survive to hold those beautiful hands in his again. He also developed a rationale that he was sent into the camps as a psychiatrist so that after his release he could later relate his findings to scientific colleagues all over the world. Perhaps this also explains how John Lahola survived the death camps. He wore a red triangle on his prison garb signifying that he was a political prisoner. Could it be that his passionate devotion to a free, independent, and democratic Ukraine helped him overcome the camp repression? After all, there was so much to endure.

Survival

On arrival at Auschwitz, each prisoner was registered and assigned a number. While two guards held the prisoner down, a third prison guard roughly tattooed this number on the prisoner's arm with three needles. The number permanently branded on John Lahola's arm was 154820, which became his new name. By the time the tattoo ordeal was over, John was drenched in blood. He was then forced to join the others, and was led to the barracks.

Silence ruled the barracks. It was clear that a complaint made within earshot of the guards meant instant death. A "punishment hole," where prisoners were beaten until dead, served as an effective reminder of the futility of complaining.

There were no beds. The prisoners were jammed together on shelves just large enough for four prisoners to lie down on their sides one way, while four laid the other way. Latrine breaks occurred only in the early morning, when the guards shouted for the inmates to get up. They then beat the prisoners to hurry them along. Next was the routine roll call in the courtyard, during which prisoners were required to stand naked, often in the snow.

Each prisoner was issued one pair of pants, one shirt, and one jacket. If a prisoner was discovered with anything else, he was beaten to death. As soon as a weaker prisoner fell, he was thrown into ice water—an instant death. By the end of each day, there was always a pile of human corpses waiting to be burned. Resistance was impossible.

For two weeks, newcomers were "initiated" into Auschwitz. First they were divided into groups of 100. Then, to induce terror and submission to camp authority, every 10th man was arbitrarily shot. Next, some of the prisoners were strapped down to benches and beaten so badly by the Gestapo that their screams didn't even sound human. At the end of each day, as the prisoners returned from backbreaking work, they were herded back into the barracks. There was always a mad rush to get inside in order to avoid the Gestapo, who would beat the stragglers. Anyone who tried to escape was found, tortured, and then paraded in front of the inmates. A sign was hung around the inmate's neck declaring, "I tried to run away but did not succeed. Hurray, I'm back!"

As the horrors of initiation to Auschwitz subsided, Lahola came face to face with an equally insidious threat to his survival: hunger. As the SS guards cut back on food rations, famine stalked the camps. In the face of death, the pursuit of any form of nourishment became a never-ending obsession. Virtually no price was too high to satisfy the hunger pangs constantly tormenting them. John's experiences vividly illustrate the magnitude of the problem.

Enforced starvation turned John into a scavenger. Whenever a camp guard threw away an empty can of food, he would scoop it up and clean it out with his fingers. Such a can meant two or three days of nourishment. Once, while searching through the personal effects of some prisoners who had been removed by the guards, John found a jar of goose fat. Over the next few days, he gleefully smeared the fat over his camp ration of bread. Fortuitously, after months on a famine diet, John was chosen by the SS to unload a bread truck. To be caught stealing bread meant instant death. Nonetheless, in an unattended moment, John devoured as much bread as he could. Then he hid more bread away in his clothing to take back to the barracks. Luckily that day, he passed through the camp gates unchecked. However, his feeble body could not process the sudden onslaught of food. John became violently ill, vomiting everything he had eaten. He was so sick he gave whatever bread he smuggled into the camp to the other inmates because he knew he wouldn't be able to eat it himself.

Liquor was obviously unavailable to prisoners in the camps. As such, it was a prized commodity, which could be traded for food. On one occasion, John was unloading wagons of goods that had been brought in from the front when he spotted a whiskey bottle. He immediately concocted a scheme to smuggle the bottle into the camp compound. He found a strap, which he tied around his waist. He then hung the bottle down his pant leg, suspended from the strap. As the prisoners marched through the camp gate, the strap broke and the bottle fell to the ground. When the guards discovered it, they halted the return of the work party. The guards demanded that the prisoner who stole the bottle step forward and confess. John stood silent, as did the others. When nobody confessed, the guards searched every prisoner, ultimately finding the strap around John's waist. They said nothing, but the next day, John was ordered to report to a hard labor work party digging ditches several kilometers away from the camp. Exhausted after two weeks, John knew that he would not last if he continued to work there.

Shortly thereafter, the camp cook chose John to help in the kitchen. He was safe and in a place where he could attend to his hunger, albeit at great risk. His main job was to fill big pots with soup for the SS officers. He would then carry the soup pots to the soldiers at meal times. He would wrap a rag around his hand to help carry the pot, and as he pretended to hurry along, would purposefully spill some of that soup on to the rag. Later, back in the barracks, he would rinse the rag into his cup and drink the dribbles of soup for extra nourishment.

Every day, for three years, John Lahola and others around him endured this torment. Every day, more people died in the gas chambers. Every day, their bodies were stripped of jewelry and gold teeth and then piled up on carts to be wheeled to the incinerators. Every night, as the prisoners of Auschwitz looked on, flames and smoke danced above the Birkenau chimney while the putrid stench of cremated bodies permeated the air. This relentless process continued, like at a huge factory, until the facilities were taxed to the limit. Toward the end, Lahola and other inmates were forced to collect firewood from the surrounding forests to be used to burn the overflow of corpses piled into ditches near the camp.

Finally, the end drew near. For months, rumors circulated in the camp that the Russian front was coming closer. Then, a huge fire was built to destroy camp papers and documents. Finally, on January 18, 1945, prison officials began removing the inmates. As a cook, John was one of the last to leave because he had to prepare meals for German soldiers from the front.

The Nazis now engaged in a frantic three-month effort to hide the prisoners, transferring them from one concentration camp to another. John and the others from his camp were forced to march westward for three days and nights until they reached the German border. There, as the men huddled together in the sleet and snow, they were loaded onto boxcars and transferred to Mauthausen, a concentration camp near Linz, Austria. Not long afterward, they were again transferred, this time to Melk, a converted army camp, where the prisoners worked in coal mines. Then they were transferred again, this time by tugboat into Germany to the Ebensee concentration camp. On May 6, 1945—Liberation Day—an American tank pulled through the gates of Ebensee, and the astonished soldiers informed the exhausted prisoners they were finally free.

Some of the prisoners went wild. In their rush to enter a bakery to get some bread, several of them were trampled to death by fellow inmates. Others died from bingeing at a time when their bodies were incapable of processing the food they hungrily consumed. The long nightmare, however, was finally over.

More than 50 years later, John Lahola, then living in Edmonton, Alberta, Canada, would still be swept up in emotion whenever he reflected on these events. More than anything, his three-year incarceration in Nazi concentration camps exemplified the fact that life requires struggle, and resignation and surrender are the surest prescriptions for death.

His experience, like that of the other survivors from the camps, demonstrated that the essence of life is not found in events that occur in our lives, which more often than not are arbitrary or accidental. Instead, John Lahola showed that the real issue is how to lead your life no matter what events life brings you. His survival depended on John dedicating himself to a larger cause—a free Ukraine, a cause that helped him find meaning in his suffering. It was this greater overarching purpose that saved John Lahola and helped him surmount the many great hardships he faced. This lesson was as true for many survivors of Nazi concentration camps like John Lahola as it is for those facing hardships in the United States and elsewhere today.

Psychologist Abraham Maslow developed a theory of human needs that held that before an individual could go about satisfying higher-level needs such as esteem, status, and self actualization, that individual would have to address lower-level needs like food, clothing, and shelter. Toward the end of his life, however, he changed his mind about this theory. Maslow realized that the highest order of need was for the individual to submerse himself or herself in a higher purpose—in effect to achieve immortality by being a member of a cause that would continue after that individual's death. This dedication to a higher cause is obviously what kept John Lahola alive and is something worthy of our attention.

There is more to life than just satisfying our basic human needs. In our case, as professionals, we can serve our society by being involved in professional organizations and in community activities. Through such endeavors, we can address our higher-level needs as Maslow identified them, and our efforts will go on long after we are gone.

Be Prepared to Make Mistakes

The only real mistake is the one from which we learn nothing.

–John Powell

Friday, October 2, 1992, is a day I will never forget. It started out innocently enough. I went to the office and did some last-minute things before leaving at 2 p.m. to pick up my mother and drive to the airport. The plan was for me to attend my 20-year law class reunion in Vancouver while my mother visited friends she had left behind some 10 years before, when she moved to Edmonton.

My mother was waiting at the entrance to her apartment building when I pulled up shortly after 2 p.m. As we drove to the airport, my mother reminded me of our running joke, which we tell whenever we travel anywhere. The joke goes like this: One day, a family of five went to the airport to catch a flight. When they arrived, the children began running around. As the wife tried to calm them down, the husband stood by, lamenting the fact that they had not brought their piano with them. Overhearing her husband, the wife turned to him and asked, "Are you crazy? We are trying to catch this flight, the kids are out of control, and you're talking about our piano?" The husband replied, "Yes, because I forgot our tickets on the piano."

Just as my mother told me that joke, guess what came to my mind: Where were *our* tickets? (Nowadays, you can simply walk into the airport terminal and print out your boarding pass from one of the computer kiosks. Back then, this was not the case!) I began frantically searching for my binder, which contained our tickets. I like to think of myself as very disciplined and organized, so it came as a real shock to me that I had forgotten our tickets at the office. We were obviously going to miss our flight, and I was going to miss an event that happens just once every 20 years.

We debated what to do next. My mother encouraged me to use a nearby payphone (back in those days, no one had mobile phones) to call the office to check whether the tickets were there. I felt too embarrassed to call, however. I said I would just drive back, grab the binder, and then see what could be done about finding an alternate flight.

Over my mother's protests, we headed back to Edmonton. I tested my minivan's reliability to the maximum in my frantic attempt to reach my office. During this trip, as any self-respecting 81-year-old mother would do, my mother repeatedly reminded me of my short-comings and concluded that my forgetfulness was directly related to my failure to listen to her. If she had been anyone else, I would not have taken the berating. But my mother—hey, she's entitled! With her, I had to grin and bear it.

Of course, my staff were no dummies. They had noticed that I had left my tickets behind. They had then contacted taxis, couriers, and the airlines, and through a superb effort had managed to get our courier service to deliver my tickets to the airport ticket counter in time for me to catch my original flight. Of course, I did not find this out until I showed up back at the office!

Again, a debate ensued about what we should do. In the end, I instructed my staff to get on the phone, tell the airline we were on our way, and make alternate arrangements. Meanwhile, I hopped back into our van and once again headed for the airport. I'm sure you can guess what we talked about on the way! Again, if she had been anyone else, I would not have taken it. But it was my mother. She was 81 years old! Besides, it was true! If I had just listened to her back at the airport, we would not have had this problem.

We sped along to the airport. I was driving as quickly as I could safely go. But we needed gas, so I stopped and bought $10 worth. My blood pressure rose as I looked down at my watch. I could hardly wait for the gas to get into the tank. We headed out while the service station attendant was still wiping off our windows and wondering what was the hurry.

While we were driving down the highway, a huge transparent plastic bag—about 10 feet high and 20 feet wide (no kidding!)—drifted across the road, blown by the wind, and came to a dead stop right in front of us. I made an instant strategic decision to drive right through it. As I did, the bag collapsed, but then latched on to our back fender. It trailed us for about five miles, fluttering wildly in the wind behind the van. No time to stop!

We pulled into the airport. The tickets were there. A new reservation got us into Vancouver with plenty of time to attend the reunion. Praise God! But I hope I never have to relive that experience. The experience did remind me, however, what is possible if you do not let mistakes stop you from getting to your goal. It also showed me what damage can be done when you are too proud to admit making a mistake! What matters in life is not how many mistakes you make, but whether you reach your goal. Never let your pride get in the way of admitting a mistake so you can move ahead.

STAND UP FOR
WHAT YOU
BELIEVE IN!

Important principles may, and must, be inflexible.

–Abraham Lincoln, 1856

Danylo Shumuk (pronounced Shoo-mook), who was for many years the world's longest imprisoned prisoner of conscience, first came to my attention in 1972, when reading a *Time* magazine article about him on a flight from Washington D.C. to New York. As I read about him, I felt that his situation seemed hopeless. I did not know then that in the years that followed, I would be drawn into a 15-year campaign to set him free. While his life has now passed into the pages of history, the principles he symbolized and lived for remain eternal, and are as true today as they were in his darkest hours.

Shumuk's life can be summed up in three words: courage, triumph, and achievement. It is my hope that in learning about Danylo Shumuk's life, you will be inspired to reflect on your own life. I hope you will paint a new portrait of yourself—one in which you are portrayed as the hero of your ideals, and in which you emerge as the champion of your freedom and your life.

On May 23, 1987, I was with a small group of dedicated people at the Calgary International Airport awaiting the arrival of Danylo Shumuk. Shumuk had endured 40 years in Soviet concentration camps before his release and arrival in Canada. He had dedicated his entire life to achieving one goal: freedom for himself, his nation, and the people of Eastern Europe and the Soviet Union. On that day, in 1987, his dream was about to be fulfilled.

As we stood in the airport hallway—maybe 50 of us, huddled tightly together—we watched in wonder as Shumuk passed through the airport gate to meet us. His wilted flesh and drawn cheeks did not prevent him from smiling as he peered out at us through his dark, sunken eyes. You could see in those eyes that he was as proud to have fought for our freedom as we were to have fought for his. As we gathered around this frail old man, his gentle spirit radiated outward, touching each of us like the glow of a campfire deep in the night. Overwhelmed with joy as we watched him being showered with greetings from family and friends, some of us began to weep gently.

Courage

Now, when I think back to that day in Calgary, I sometimes wonder how Shumuk felt when he arrived in Canada. I wonder what thoughts went through his mind. Of course, we will never really know. But, certainly, one of the things he was facing was the great cultural transition from Eastern Europe to North America. As someone of Eastern European heritage, I could understand. But surely, he must also have reflected on his life story.

His story began in Eastern Europe in 1914, in the village of Boremschyna, located in what is now Ukraine. As a young man, Shumuk became a devout communist. In January of 1929, Shumuk was arrested for his underground activities in Western Ukraine. In his memoirs, he wrote:

> I was a communist, an idealist. I was the kind of communist who was prepared to go to jail for his ideals, but not the kind of communist who, today, is prepared to put other people in jail for their convictions. Yet, still, I was a communist, and in this I was mistaken, and for this I must bear part of the responsibility for the great tragedies that have befallen my people.

With the outset of World War II, following a general amnesty that led to his release, Shumuk was conscripted into the Red Army and sent to the Western Front. His entire military unit was encircled by the Germans, but he managed to escape and make his way back to his native village. During this journey, his encounters with ordinary, common, salt-of-the-Earth people changed him. It was a pivotal time in his life.

Shumuk had long heard of Stalinist atrocities, such as the 1933 state-imposed artificial famine, a genocide that killed some 7 million people. But it wasn't until Shumuk's journey that he became convinced of the truth of these events. Two stories stood out in particular.

In one, a man named Pavlo Kulyk related how, as a young boy, his mother tied his foot to the kitchen table to prevent him from crawling out into the streets where famished peasants roamed, scooping up little children to eat in face of the horrific famine. In another, an elderly couple related how they had scoured barren fields in search of gopher and mice holes. The little animals were known for keeping food stashes, which the elderly couple would find to eat and stave off hunger. Such stories—and the tens, hundreds, and even thousands like them—forced Shumuk to face a moment of truth. He turned his back on his communist ideology and instead embraced the goal of establishing a free and democratic state.

Shumuk's dream was born. It was to gain freedom for himself without compromising his human dignity, to gain freedom for his nation without compromising its national character, to gain freedom for all the people of Eastern Europe without compromising their rights—and indirectly, to gain freedom for you and me.

In his memoirs, Shumuk wrote, "I have always known that my place under any totalitarian society is in the concentration camp." And verily, it was.

Consider the following events:

  ❖ The West sinks into the great depression of the 1920s.
  ❖ Hitler rises to power in Nazi Germany in the 1930s.
  ❖ Poland is divided between Nazi Germany and the Soviet Union in 1939.
  ❖ World War II occurs.
  ❖ The United States drops atomic bombs on Nagasaki and Hiroshima in Japan in 1945.

❖ The Korean War occurs.

❖ Nikita Khrushchev rises to power in the Soviet Union in the 1950s.

❖ Construction of the Berlin Wall begins in 1961.

❖ The Vietnam War occurs.

❖ Nelson Mandela is arrested in South Africa in 1962.

❖ President Kennedy is assassinated in 1963.

❖ U.S. President Richard Nixon resigns in 1974 following the Watergate scandal.

❖ Anatoly Sharansky is arrested in the Soviet Union in 1977.

❖ John Lennon is assassinated in the streets of New York in 1980.

❖ The space shuttle *Challenger* explodes on liftoff in 1986.

❖ A catastrophic nuclear accident occurs in Chernobyl in 1986.

Through all of these events, Danylo Shumuk languished in Soviet concentration camps not for what he did, but for the ideals of democracy and freedom that he symbolized. Indeed, for four long decades, under the Soviet Union, Shumuk sat behind barbed wires and watchtowers at a time when every minute, every second, seemed to last eternally. While his supporters sought his freedom, Western leaders ignored him. Instead, at summit after summit, these leaders sought to make peace and find accommodation with his tormentors as countless others followed him into the gulag and prisons elsewhere.

In December 1972, after Shumuk had already spent more than 25 years in Soviet concentration camps, news of his incarceration reached the West when the aforementioned *Time* magazine published a story about his life. A campaign to secure his release gained momentum when Amnesty International, the worldwide human rights organization, declared him to be the world's longest imprisoned prisoner of conscience. In the years that followed, many voices joined in the campaign to set him free.

In the United States, then-Senator (and later Republican presidential candidate) Robert Dole and others wrote letters to Soviet leader Leonid Brezhnev on his behalf. In Canada, Parliament passed a unanimous resolution calling for Shumuk's release. Joe Clark, then Minister of External Affairs and a former Prime Minister, began working on the campaign. Former Soviet dissident Eduard Kuznetsov (in Israel) and former Red Army General Petro Hryhorenko (in New York) issued pleas on Shumuk's behalf. Over the next 15 years, this international campaign, held together by a string of volunteers from the United States, Canada, South America, Europe, Israel, and Japan, worked tirelessly on Shumuk's behalf to set him free.

But it was all in vain. In vain, telegrams and letters were sent to the Kremlin. In vain, petitions with thousands of signatures were gathered on his behalf. In vain, numerous interventions by diplomats with Soviet counterparts called for his release. In his late 60s, plagued with stomach illness and internal bleeding, Shumuk turned to face this, his final sprint, alone. Even his most ardent supporters, including myself, had given up all hope.

Triumph

Suddenly, just when all hope was lost, the Kremlin relented and announced that Shumuk would be set free and allowed to emigrate to the West. As I mentioned, he arrived in Canada on May 23, 1987.

In what sometimes seems like a sea of human mediocrity, Danylo Shumuk stood out as a moral giant. His release cast a ray of hope onto millions of souls living in chains, reaffirming to them that their suffering was not forlorn and that someday soon it too would end. His triumph was a triumph for all people who love freedom or yearn for it. His victory was a victory of lifelong dedication, and a victory of the human spirit.

In the summer of 1987, following Shumuk's arrival in the West, I accompanied him to the American Bar Association convention in San Francisco. This trip helped me gain some insights into his life. He was a deeply compassionate leader and a tender human being. But he was also quite a character.

For one thing, he enjoyed drinking a Coca Cola first thing in the morning. I suppose after 40 years in jail, he was entitled to this eccentricity. He was a free spirit. Sometimes, he would charge out somewhere without telling anyone where he was going, but he would always soon return. He explained that sitting in jail cells made him particularly appreciative of the ability to take off whenever he wanted to. He knew how to get along with people, respected their opinions, and was curious to hear their views even on matters in which he was obviously the expert. He also especially enjoyed humor.

People often asked him the difference between the Soviet Union and the United States. He replied, "The constitution of the Soviet Union and the United States guarantee freedom of speech. But only the American constitution guarantees freedom *after* speech."

When asked to compare the lives of prisoners in the Soviet Union with prisoners in America. He stated, "Prisoners in the United States sometimes write books *after* jail, while prisoners in the Soviet Union usually write books *before* jail."

He held American attorneys in the highest regard and understood the vital role they play in protecting the rule of law and the rights of ordinary people. In his remarks at the American Bar Association meeting, he underlined that it was important for the legal profession to guard against attempts to belittle its value and equate it with others in other countries that would have the world believe they are fulfilling the same role as "attorneys." His intervention with the American Bar Association turned out to be successful.

Achievement

In the years that followed, Danylo Shumuk would observe the great global transformation to which he had dedicated his life. He would see the demise of the Soviet Empire and its threat to world peace. He would witness the creation of a new world order in which his people and millions of others would find their freedom and independence. In short, he would achieve his dream of freedom. Shumuk died a free man in 2004, and was buried in his native and free Ukraine.

If your life is like mine, you will find that at times, it will pass by you like a hurricane. In those moments, your values and what you stand for will keep you anchored. Draw from Shumuk's example in leading your life by fearlessly acknowledging the truth and fighting for your beliefs without compromising your principles.

TRUST YOUR INSTINCTS

Ideas pull the trigger, but instinct loads the gun.

–Don Marquis

In March of 1996, while living in Canada, I visited my 86-year-old aunt Helen in Los Angeles after taking a brief trip in Phoenix. As I lay in bed after spending the day with her, I looked at my watch. It was 11:10 p.m. I went back to reflecting on the action-filled day we had just enjoyed. I was tired. But suddenly, I became alarmed. I looked at my watch again. The date showed March 8, 1996. Was that right? I asked myself.

It seemed to me that I was scheduled to leave Los Angeles for Canada on March 9. I looked at my plane ticket. Sure enough, I was scheduled to depart on a Canada 3000 flight on March 9, at 12:55 a.m. Wait a minute! March 9 at 12:55 a.m.? That was less than two hours away! Somehow, it just didn't seem right. But my watch showed March 8. In less than an hour, it would be March 9.

I couldn't just pick up and leave. What was I supposed to do? Should I announce in a quick sweep through the house, while picking up my belongings, that it was nice visiting, but I've got to go? What kind of guest would do that? How was my elderly aunt, who saw me maybe once a year for a few days, supposed to react to that? Still, the fact remained that unless I left immediately, I would miss my plane.

I leaped out of bed. Frantically, I started stuffing my clothes into my suitcase. Running around the house like a chicken with its head cut off, I collected everything I needed, announced that I had to leave, and soothed my dear aunt's dismay as much as I could in three minutes. I jammed my suitcase into the rental car, kissed my aunt goodbye, and hopped into the driver's seat. The thought that this might be the last time I see my aunt entered my mind. As I said goodbye, I felt like this wasn't the way I should be going. But what could I do? I roared off in the darkness, flicking my headlights to signal my goodbye.

I raced to the freeway, moved to the fast lane, and peeled off toward city center. Luckily, traffic was sparse because it was late. I passed car after car, as if I were trying to set a new world speed record. Moving from the Pasadena Freeway to the Harbor Freeway was no problem. The customary traffic delays associated with the merger of these two freeways were minimal. I was making good time and actually thought I would make it.

I turned off on the Century Boulevard exit. Whistling through Inglewood and into the LAX airport area, I searched for the Thrifty Car Rental location. It was to my left, but looked dark and closed. I pulled a U-turn and drove right into their garage. There was nobody around, so I just left the keys on the seat along with a filled out rental agreement. No problem! Now all I had to do was figure out how to get to the terminal from there.

Just then, a bus pulled up, dropping off a load of Thrifty passengers. I jumped on board and looked at my watch. It was 12:15 a.m. I grabbed the bus driver, a thin, scraggly looking man, and barked out instructions about getting me to the Tom Bradley International Terminal right away or I'd miss my flight. Then I flopped onto a seat. Luckily, my concern and anxiety set the driver on fire. He ripped past a dozen terminals, ignoring passengers trying to flag him down, to get me where I was going on time. Thanking him profusely for his courage and dedication, I hopped off the bus, scooped up my bags, and ran inside.

"Quick!" I thought. "Where's Canada 3000?" It was 12:30 a.m. Would I make it? A small sign pointed to the Canada 3000 aisle. I ran into the aisle, up one side and down the other. No Canada 3000! I looked at my ticket again. I noticed that it was in a Fiesta Travel jacket. Maybe it's Fiesta Airlines? I ran back to the main directory board, but there was no Fiesta Airlines! There was just Canada 3000.

The terminal is dead. I mean, there was hardly anyone except for a huge lineup of Mexicans headed for Guadalajara or somewhere on Mexican Airlines. The only other guy around who could speak English was mopping the floor.

"Where is Canada 3000?" I asked him. He looked up and pointed in the direction of another aisle. I rushed off to the aisle he pointed at, but there was no Canada 3000. Okay, where was Canada 3000? Not down aisle one, not down aisle two. Could it be down aisle three? I zipped down aisle number three. There was no Canada 3000, no Fiesta Airlines—nothing, except a Canadian Airlines ticket counter. There was only one problem: Nobody was there!

I banged on the counter. Maybe there was someone in the back! But no luck. Just then, a Canadian Airlines ticket agent entered the aisle headed in my direction. Accosting her, I pulled out my ticket and I hopefully asked, "Where's Canada 3000? My plane leaves in 20 minutes." The agent looked at the ticket and said, "This says you are leaving March 9." I said, "Yes, March 9." Then I looked at my watch. The calendar said March 8! No! No! I looked again— March 8! How could that be? It said March 8 at 11:10, when I was at my aunt's house. It was now after midnight, meaning it should now say March 9!

Then I realized what had happened.

When I was in Phoenix, the time was one hour ahead of Los Angeles. My calendar had been set to Phoenix time. As a result, it had already flipped the date to March 8 when I checked my watch at my aunt's house. In fact, in Los Angeles, it was still March 7. I was reading the watch correctly, but the watch wasn't properly set.

I thought, "Now what should I do?" I felt like a complete idiot. I called my aunt Helen and arranged to go back to her place. The following day, we went to Santa Monica, where we spent a beautiful, leisurely afternoon together. In the evening, I said my proper goodbyes before I left.

In my career, there have been times, as in this story, when I was *sure* I was right about something, and was prepared to stake everything on it. For example, I have participated in trials when I was certain we would win or made investments that I just knew would be good. Then, despite my best efforts, things did not turn out the way they should have. These times, and this story, remind us that we are not infallible. You simply have to be prepared to deal with life as it presents itself, for better or for worse.

In Dark Moments Remember the "Why" of Your Life

We shall draw from the heart of suffering itself the means of inspiration and survival.

–Winston Churchill

Sometimes, while pursuing your career, you may get so involved in the "what" that you are doing that you lose sight of the "why." As Peter Lowe, a prominent motivational speaker points out, even if you may not always be content with your work, you can find fulfillment in recalling why you are working—for example, because you are supporting your family.

The following true story underlines the fact that as human beings, we find meaning in our lives through our relationships with others.

On the night of July 30, 1945, two weeks before the end of the war, while sailing from Guam to Leyte, the Navy Cruiser *USS Indianapolis* was torpedoed by a Japanese submarine. The crew of 1,199 men ended up in the waters of the Pacific. So began one of the most incredible stories of World War II. Oral histories of survivors published by the Naval Historical Center of the U.S. Department of the Navy describe the amazing events that followed. Of particular interest is the interview with Captain Charles B. McVay who was the commanding officer of the ship.

On Sunday night, the 29th of July…approximately five minutes after midnight [on 30 July], I was thrown from my emergency cabin bunk on the bridge by a very violent explosion followed shortly thereafter by another explosion. I went to the bridge and noticed, in my emergency cabin and charthouse, that there was quite a bit of acrid white smoke. I couldn't see anything…. I asked the officer of the deck [the senior officer on duty] if he had had any reports. He said "No, sir. I have lost all communications."…

Within another two or three minutes the executive officer [the second in command on the ship] came up…and said, "We are definitely going down and I suggest that we abandon ship."…

As I had this word passed, I turned to the officer of the deck…and said, "I have been unable to determine whether the distress message, which I told the navigator to check on, has ever gotten out."…

I was sucked off into the water by what I believe was a wave caused by the bow going down rather rapidly….

Within a few seconds, I felt hot oil and water brush over the back of my neck and looked around and heard a swish and the ship was gone….We could still see nothing. It was still dark and I could hear people yelling for help….

Most people had been sucked down by the ship or were full of fuel oil and salt water and were violently ill or else so exhausted that they lay more or less in a stupor….Their eyes were filled with fuel oil and consequently, they spent a very uncomfortable 36 to 48 hours trying to get the fuel oil out….

The first night, the first day, Monday, and Tuesday night, were, as I say, very uncomfortable. We then had two days of almost no wind and a glassy [calm] sea. However, the sea still contained those long rolling swells which did not permit you to see very far….

The interesting point to me is that we should have been so far north of the large group of survivors, which I will call the life preserver group, as those people, hundreds of them, had nothing at all except life preservers. Some of them didn't even have a life preserver….

The people who were in this group had mass hallucinations. One of the stories is that three or four people would swim away at dark and the next morning they'd come back and say, "Why, the *Indianapolis* didn't go down after all. She is just over there and we were on her all night. We got fresh milk, we got tomato juice, we got water."…

> It was in that way that so many people apparently died of exhaustion. Either that or else they drank salt water and went completely out of their head....
>
> The people that were down in that group feel quite sure that a number of people just gave up hope because they were with the bunch at sundown and in the morning they would be gone, so they feel that people just slipped out of their life jackets and just decided that they didn't want to face it any longer....
>
> The group down there said that on calm days, they knew there were sharks around because they could see them underneath.

According to testimony given from other survivors, hundreds of sharks emerged and circled them. As the sharks attacked, the once-optimistic men were filled with a sense of vulnerability and helplessness. Each day, the sharks would attack in the morning, cruise through the wounded and dying all day, and then feed on the living again at night.

According to the book *In Harm's Way* by Doug Stanton, as time passed, each man, during moments of lucidity, had to ask himself the same hard question: Will I live or do I quit? At some point, each survivor made a vow to himself: *I am going to live.* Some, who did not give up hope, started betting who would survive the longest. They started remembering people back home who had told them in words or deeds never to give up. They assured themselves and each other that rescue was imminent. They prayed aloud. They made deals with God, promising to read the Bible, to write to their parents more, to never cheat, if only they could survive this day.

Returning to the closing part of Captain McVay's statement:

> To give some explanation as to how we were picked up and when, I talked to the aviator, Lt. Wilbur C. Gwinn...who was piloting...a [PV-1] patrol bomber....He...was on a regular routine reconnaissance and search from Palau when he...went back to take a Loran [navigational] fix...and happened to glance down towards the water and saw a large oil slick.
>
> He then decreased his altitude and followed the oil slick for a number of miles when he sighted the group of what he thought were about 30 survivors. He did not know that they were survivors from the *Indianapolis*. He did not know the *Indianapolis* was missing.

This was...Thursday, 2 August, that he sighted these survivors....He then, an hour later, sighted another group of survivors and sent a message—

"Send rescue...150 survivors in life boat and jackets."...

The long nightmare was over. Upon completion of the search on August 8, 1945, 316 men were rescued out of the crew of 1,199. The men had survived by helping each other and by vowing to live for others: God, their sweethearts and wives, their parents, and their children. Their story underlines the fact that if you are ever called upon to take heroic measures to survive, even if you cannot do so for yourself, more likely than not, you will find the strength to do so for the sake of those you love. Truly they can provide you with the "why" of your life in moments of weakness when you cannot find it from within yourself.

PARTING
THOUGHTS

When you were born, you cried while everyone else rejoiced.
Lead your life in such a way that when you die you
rejoice while everyone else cries.

–Native American saying

You were brought into this world and given life. Call it the work of God, divine providence, or destiny; regardless, it was not your decision. However, once you arrived, it became up to you to learn how to live. Your happiness, health and prosperity are up to you.

More than anything, I hope this book helps you in enhancing your life. I hope the stories I've shared will help you find the courage to try your best in life. I hope you will come to know the joy of triumph. And I hope this book will help you lead a life of achievement.

Let me conclude with this story. For many years, a dusty pebble lay on the side of a dirt road, unnoticed by hundreds of passers-by who traveled that way each day. Then, one day, an old man walking down the roadway noticed the stone and immediately recognized it for what it was. He quickly grabbed the pebble and scooped it into his pocket. Later that night, while at home, he pulled out the stone and polished it with a rag. As the old man worked, cleaning off the dirt and the dust, the pebble began to glow and then shine. It soon turned into what it really was: a diamond that reflected the light from the lantern into the brilliant colors of the rainbow on the walls.

As the old man looked at the precious gem, he began to think about its creation—about how it was formed beneath the Earth's crust, where high temperatures and pressure caused the diamond to crystallize. He thought about how the diamond was later brought to the Earth's surface by violent volcanic activity erupting through the Earth's crust.

He observed the unique features of the diamond. He thought of its great power to bend rays of light, breaking them up into beautiful colors. He thought about the highly trained workers who took many years to learn their trade, applying their skills to cut and polish the rough diamond in a slow and costly process to create the beautiful gem that it was.

We are all like that pebble lying on the side of the road, waiting for someone to come along and recognize the beauty within us. We all hope to be discovered by someone who will apply a little polish to bring out the luster inside. We all have to undergo the tests of life in the same way that the diamond was formed and crystallized by high temperatures and pressure.

We are also like that diamond in the sense that we can reflect the light, beauty, and experiences that we encounter in our lives. We are like that diamond in the sense that our parents and family applied many years of care in the slow and costly process of raising us from children to adults.

What is even more important, however, is for us to realize that we are also capable of recognizing the beauty in others. We are capable of helping others through the challenges of life, of pointing out the beauty of life to others and contributing to the slow and demanding process of raising children. In this way, we are all able, through a little work and caring for the people around us, to bring out the true value and worth in them.

My best wishes for you,

Andy J. Semotiuk

Index

HERE IS WHAT PROFESSIONALS ARE SAYING ABOUT THIS BOOK

"An engaging and entertaining presentation of real-life lessons every young health professional needs to know."

–Gerri Nakonechny, Former Dean of Health and Community Studies, Grant MacEwan College, Edmonton, Alberta, Canada

"An exceptional resource for teachers and all professionals seeking the formula for success and balance in life."

–Susan Dunn, Teacher, Phoenix, Arizona

"This book is an excellent tool for young accountants."

–Hank Anding, CPA, JD, H&R Block Premium, Glendale, California

"I believe this book will be very useful to young engineers."

–Mike Moros, Engineer, Etobicoke, Ontario, Canada

"Andy writes for those who wish to avoid mistakes as they plan their careers. I enjoyed reading this book and I am sure you will benefit from its wisdom."

–Jaroslaw Pikolycky, DDS (licensed to practice dentistry in Great Britain, Bermuda, New York and California), La Jolla, California

"This is a great book for young architects."

–Gary Danylchuk, Architect, Lethbridge, Alberta, Canada